The Black Arts Movement

Lucent Library of Black History

Other titles in this series:

African American Folklore

The African American Religious Experience

The Atlantic Slave Trade

Black Nationalism

Blacks in Film

Blacks in Political Office

The Civil War and Emancipation

Reconstruction

Reparations for Slavery

Rosa Parks and the Montgomery Bus Boycott

The Black Arts Movement

Lucent Library of Black History

David Robson

LUCENT BOOKS
A part of Gale, Cengage Learning

 GALE
CENGAGE Learning™

Detroit • New York • San Francisco • New Haven, Conn • Waterville, Maine • London

LIBRARY OF CONGRESS CATALOGING-IN-PUBLICATION DATA

Robson, David, 1966–
  Black arts movement / by David Robson.
      p. cm. — (Lucent library of black history)
  Includes bibliographical references and index.
  ISBN 978-1-4205-0053-0 (hardcover)
  1. Black Arts movement. 2. Black nationalism—United States—History—20th century. I. Title.
  NX512.3.A35R63 2009
  700.89'96073--dc22

                                                      2008016446

Lucent Books
27500 Drake Rd.
Farmington Hills, MI 48331

ISBN-13: 978-1-4205-0053-0
ISBN-10: 1-4205-0053-8

Printed in the United States of America
1 2 3 4 5 6 7 12 11 10 09 08

Contents

Foreword   6

Introduction
"Recapture Our Heritage"   8

Chapter One
The Roots of Black Nationalism   12

Chapter Two
The Rise of the Black Arts Movement   28

Chapter Three
Cultural Influences and Identity   43

Chapter Four
Assimilation or Self-Determination?   56

Chapter Five
Black Arts Hit the Mainstream   69

Epilogue
Legacy   83

Notes   89
For More Information   94
Index   97
Picture Credits   104
About the Author   104

Foreword

It has been more than 500 years since Africans were first brought to the New World in shackles, and over 140 years since slavery was formally abolished in the United States. Over 50 years have passed since the fallacy of "separate but equal" was obliterated in the American courts, and some 40 years since the watershed Civil Rights Act of 1965 guaranteed the rights and liberties of all Americans, especially those of color. Over time, these changes have become celebrated landmarks in American history. In the twenty-first century, African American men and women are politicians, judges, diplomats, professors, deans, doctors, artists, athletes, business owners, and home owners. For many, the scars of the past have melted away in the opportunities that have been found in contemporary society. Observers such as Peter N. Kirsanow, who sits on the U.S. Commission of Civil Rights, point to these accomplishments and conclude, "The growing black middle class may be viewed as proof that most of the civil rights battles have been won."

In spite of these legal victories, however, prejudice and inequality have persisted in American society. In 2003, African Americans comprised just 12 percent of the nation's population, yet accounted for 44 percent of its prison inmates and 24 percent of its poor. Racially motivated hate crimes continue to appear on the pages of major newspapers in many American cities. Furthermore, many African Americans still experience either overt or muted racism in their daily lives. A 1996 study undertaken by Professor Nancy Krieger of the Harvard School of Public Health, for example, found that 80 percent of the African American participants reported having experienced racial discrimination in one or more settings, including at work or school, applying for housing and medical care, from the police or in the courts, and on the street or in a public setting.

It is for these reasons that many believe the struggle for racial equality and justice is far from over. These episodes of discrimination threaten to shatter the illusion that America has completely overcome its racist past, causing many black Americans to become increasingly frustrated and confused. Scholar and writer Ellis Cose has described this splintered state in the following way: "I have done everything I was supposed to do. I have stayed out of trouble with the law, gone to the right schools, and worked myself nearly to death. What more do they want? Why in God's name won't they accept me as a full human being?" For Cose and others, the struggle for equality and justice has yet to be fully achieved.

In many subtle yet important ways the traumatic experiences of slavery and segregation continue to inform the way race is discussed and experienced in the twenty-first century. Indeed, it is possible that America will always grapple with the fallout from its distressing past. Ulric Haynes, dean of the Hofstra University School of Business has said, "Perhaps race will always matter, given the historical circumstances under which we came to this country." But studying this past and understanding how it contributes to present-day dialogues about race and history in America is a critical component of contemporary education. To this end, the Lucent Library of Black History offers a thorough look at the experiences that have shaped the black community and the American people as a whole. Annotated bibliographies provide readers with ideas for further research, while fully documented primary and secondary source quotations enhance the text. Each book in the series explores a different episode of black history; together they provide students with a wealth of information as well as launching points for further study and discussion.

Introduction

"Recapture Our Heritage"

Legend has it that on the day Malcolm X died the black arts movement was born. On Sunday, February 21, 1965, the former convict and controversial civil rights icon Malcolm X was scheduled to speak at New York City's Audubon Ballroom. Only a week before, Malcolm X's family home had been firebombed; his pregnant wife, Betty, and four young children barely escaped with their lives. For two years Malcolm X had told the media that his life was in grave danger, yet the outspoken leader refused to back down.

Whether speaking out against white racism or, more recently, the corruption of his former organization, the Nation of Islam, Malcolm X tempted fate daily. His willingness to consider violence and separation from white America in the struggle for racial equality contrasted sharply with the philosophy of the Reverend Dr. Martin Luther King Jr. King, the brilliant and outspoken leader of the civil right movement, preached a message of nonviolence and integration. But like many in the African American community, Malcolm X believed King and his movement were too willing to compromise on important issues with a white establishment that blacks viewed as racist.

While in jail years before, Malcolm X had discovered Islam. He had also discovered books. From books he learned of the tortured history of African Americans. "I will never forget how shocked I was when I began reading about slavery's total horror," he wrote in his autobiography. "The world's most monstrous crime, the sin and blood on the white man's hands, are almost impossible to believe."[1]

It was, he said, essential for black people to reconnect with their proud past, a past rooted in the traditions of their African heritage, a past that had been stolen from them. Thus, a year before his untimely death, standing before an audience in Harlem, Malcolm X exhorted blacks to rediscover themselves. "We must recapture our heritage and our identity if we are ever to liberate ourselves from the bonds of white supremacy," he said. His recipe would empower a movement: "We must launch a cultural revolution to *unbrainwash* an entire people."[2]

Over the next decade, an underground movement of writers, painters, poets, and musicians would rise to take the fallen leader's words to heart. The black arts movement would one day sprout in almost every corner of the United States, with its new leaders encouraging a return to the past for inspiration. They would also encourage political action.

In time, the movement would be criticized by whites and blacks alike for its refusal to stand down and for its exclusion of white culture and influence. And then, just as the black arts movement began taking hold, it virtually disappeared.

What Was the Black Arts Movement?

Considered the artistic branch of the black power movement, the black arts movement attempted to create the cultural revolution Malcolm X spoke of. Black power, a strain of black nationalism, evolved on a parallel track with the American civil rights movement. But its ideas and tactics were considered more radical and less peaceful than those of the civil rights movement, which stressed nonviolence. If Martin Luther King Jr. was the spokesperson for mainstream civil rights, then the equally eloquent Malcolm X spoke for black nationalists.

Although black artists and publications began thriving years earlier, the time clock for the black arts movement began running the day of Malcolm X's assassination. Those artists and thinkers sympathetic to Malcolm X's ideas were outraged, though perhaps

Malcolm X talks to black Muslims at a Harlem restaurant about his ideas to help blacks rediscover themselves.

not surprised, by his murder. Collectively, they determined to carry on his ideas of separatism and revolution.

The black arts movement was large and complex. Members carried no identification cards, and there were no monthly meetings. Yet African American artists of the time were provoked and inspired by a sense of growing cultural identity. In that sense, it was a movement that moved people. Musicians, sculptors, poets, painters, novelists, and playwrights led the charge. While they worked sometimes thousands of miles apart, in groups or alone, what unified them was a desire to change American life forever—and to do it on their own terms.

Why Was It Important?

The black arts movement was a cultural landmark in American history. It paved the way for diversity in American arts and popular culture and broadened acceptance of minority voices in the visual, literary, and performing arts. It also recognized, says scholar

James Edward Smethurst, that "African Americans had a common history and a distinct national culture."[3]

This recognition was essential because black culture was typically deemed inferior to that of whites. The black arts movement began transforming this view from the inside out. It encouraged self-reliance, political engagement, and a break from a white culture that continually rejected it. "Its function," writes critic Henry Louis Gates, "was to serve the political liberation of black people from white racism."[4]

Although the movement lasted only a decade and ended in 1975, black arts helped transform the notion of what it means to be an African American. Its words, music, and images cast a shadow that is still visible in the twenty-first century.

How Does It Influence American Culture Today?

Although the black arts movement ended in 1975, its influence on black artists did not.

Art created by African Americans is more popular than ever before. The cultural avalanche of black art, so long in coming, arrived like a thunderstorm and is still with us.

From the prize-winning jazz compositions of Wynton Marsalis to the provocative films of Spike Lee; from the streetwise rap of Public Enemy to the lyrical prose of Edward P. Jones, the revolution is televised around the world every day and blasted from millions of car speakers. "It's not that there are black artists and intellectuals who matter," say Gates. "It's that so many artists and intellectuals who matter are black."[5] The difference, he suggests, is one of influence and acceptance, not despite racial differences but because of them.

Chapter One

The Roots of Black Nationalism

Black nationalism is the idea that black people share a common identity and destiny. It hinges on the principles of racial pride and independence from white society. While black nationalism first took root in the late nineteenth century, the painful history of slavery and the subsequent political and social oppression of African Americans in North America is crucial in understanding black nationalism and, subsequently, the black arts movement.

In their brutal journey from small villages in western Africa to the shores of the American colonies—later known as the United States—enslaved black people lost more than their freedom. They also lost their native cultures. Forced to abide by the rules of their captors, African Americans were shorn of their past and, consequently, their identity. It would take hundreds of years and the vision of great artists, thinkers, and revolutionaries to begin taking it back.

Living a Nightmare

During the height of the transatlantic slave trade, from the 1500s through the 1860s, roughly 15 million Africans were sold into slavery around the world. Today the American descendants of slaves number 40 million. The story of the slave trade is one of suffering and death.

The journey into slavery could take months, as war prisoners, refugees, and other unlucky individuals in countries such as Sierra Leone and Ghana were captured and bound at the neck with rope or chains. Next came the backbreaking "Long March"—perhaps 300 miles (483km)—from the interior of the country to the sea, where a cargo ship waited along the coast. Because slave ships often stopped at many ports to capture and shackle more slaves, the infamous Middle Passage could take up to ten months.

The average slave ship held 350 Africans. Below deck, men were chained flat in pairs in spaces 16 inches (40.6cm) wide and 5 feet (1.5m) long. Women and children remained unchained and were allowed occasionally to roam the deck. The conditions were horrendous. Nigerian Olaudah Equino, who went on to write the first slave narrative in the late 1700s, spoke of the smells

Slave ships transported an average of 350 Africans each under horrendous conditions during the slave trade as this eighteenth-century engraving depicts.

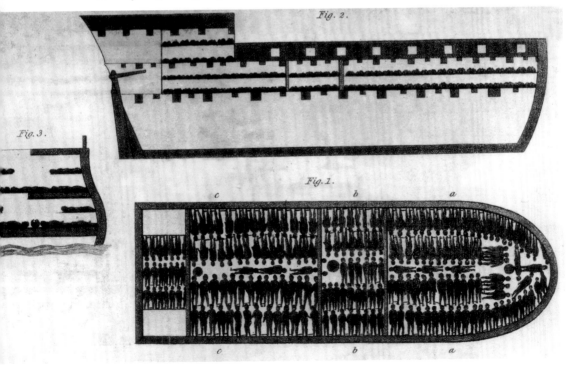

and sounds: "The stench of the hold . . . became pestilential," he wrote. "The shrieks of the women, and the groans of the dying, rendered the whole a scene of horror."[6] Although Equino survived his ordeal, he never forgot the experience.

Those slaves who arrived alive on the other side of the world staggered from the ship's hold sick and debilitated, only to be sold to owners who often mistreated them and separated them from their families. Although officially banned in 1808, the Atlantic slave trade did not truly end in the United States until 1859. After nearly three hundred years, slaves remained deprived of their native languages and customs

Emancipation in 1863 and the end of the Civil War in 1865 did little to improve the everyday lives of African Americans. Between 1877 and the early 1970s, southern Jim Crow laws kept blacks and whites separated. Some of these laws were enforced by local, state, and federal governments; others simply existed out of custom. Writer Charles George explains: "Since blacks were never considered equal to whites, they were expected to call all whites 'master' and 'mistress,' speak only when spoken to, and never look a white person directly in the eye. Thus, a tradition of control of one race by another was established."[7]

Marcus Garvey and the Call Home

As the twentieth century dawned, a number of voices began crying out for respect. In fits and starts, African American leaders like Booker T. Washington and W.E.B. DuBois charted a course toward reconciliation with whites. Principally, the call was for integration; blacks and whites would be treated equally in all facets of American life. But this proved unrealistic to many Americans.

For its part, much of black America craved leadership it could relate to and understand. The time was right for a national movement—one that promoted racial pride and change. The time was right for outspoken, rabble-rousing leadership of the kind that Marcus Garvey specialized in.

While growing up in Saint Anne's Bay, Jamaica, Garvey rarely saw the ugly side of racism. His family was far from rich, but they never went hungry. Garvey's father worked as a mason, while his mother raised crops to sell and for the family's dinner table. One of his best friends, Joyce Rerrie, was a white girl; neither child ever questioned the color of each other's skin. They only knew that they enjoyed playing games and spending time with one another.

When Marcus and Joyce became teenagers, everything changed. Joyce was sent to England at the age of fourteen; her father warned her to stay away from Marcus because he was a "nigger."[8] For the first time in his young life, Marcus was forced to confront his race. "He felt shut out," says writer Robert Hill. "He felt that he was excluded and made to feel that he was not good enough, and the rest of his life was really an attempt to prove that he was just as good as anyone else in the world."[9]

As he grew to adulthood, Garvey developed his reading, writing, and speaking skills. He bet friends that they could not find one word in the dictionary that he did not know. He dreamed of becoming a great man, a leader, but he knew tiny Saint Anne's Bay would only hold him back.

In 1910, barely into his twenties, Garvey traveled to Central America, working as a journalist and day laborer along the way.

Slave Art: The Resistance Begins

Like members of the black arts movement centuries later, slaves used their art for practical purposes. Slave songs, or spirituals, handmade quilts, and poetry did more than express a link to slaves' African past; they often contained coded messages. One spiritual, called "Steal Away," exhorts its listeners to quietly escape from bondage. Popular quilting patterns included the "Flying Geese" and the instructional "North Star," a heavenly guidepost for escapees. Such patterns might be hung outside a slave's quarters as a signal to others looking to run away.

Before and during the Civil War, abolitionists published slave poems in their newspapers as a way of gaining members. The poems themselves often report on the dreadful conditions of slaves, including long hours in the hot sun and daily whippings. Despite the practical and secretive nature of slave art, care had to be taken. Owners usually viewed communication between slaves as a danger to their valuable property. They also frowned on teaching slaves to read. After all, as writer and orator Frederick Douglass suggested, an educated slave is less likely to want to remain a slave.

During his travels he witnessed firsthand the bloody legacy of colonialism. For most native peoples, their countries were not their own; instead, European powers controlled the natural resources and, thus, the wealth.

Far from Jamaica, Garvey saw men and women, dark skinned like him, toiling for little money on plantations and on the greatest engineering marvel of its time, the Panama Canal. These people were powerless. Garvey decided this had to change.

Garvey's mother had wanted to name him Moses, after the biblical hero who had led the Israelites out of slavery. And as he matured, Garvey, too, began seeing himself as a leader of people. Upon returning to Jamaica he got to work. Inspired, he said, by

Marcus Garvey, who organized the Universal Negro Improvement Association in 1914, is considered the founder of black nationalism.

the book *Up from Slavery* by American Booker T. Washington, Garvey founded the Universal Negro Improvement Association (UNIA) in 1914. The goal of the organization was to lift blacks up, give them something—and someone—to believe in. In Garvey's words the UNIA was founded to "unite all the Negro peoples of the world into one great body to establish a country and government absolutely their own."[10]

Yet in Garvey's homeland, the UNIA quickly ran aground. Despite his personal charisma and passion, Garvey also had a talent for making enemies. He attacked local leaders, was intolerant of other ideas, and misused UNIA contributions earmarked for a school. Soon after, he left Jamaica again, this time under less pleasant circumstances.

Garvey's New Audience

Despite his mistakes Garvey marched on. In 1916 he arrived in New York City. Though penniless, he determined to remake himself and spread his nationalistic vision. For a time he lived with a Jamaican family, working in a print shop by day, speaking to those who would listen by night. He started on street corners and before long was drawing larger and larger crowds. Urban blacks clamored for strong and revolutionary leadership, and soon Garvey's ideas of racial pride and self-determination caught fire. "Be as proud of your race today as our fathers were in the days of yore," said Garvey. "We have a beautiful history. And we shall create another in the future that will astonish the world."[11] With words like these, considered radical in their time, Garvey's UNIA would capture the imaginations of African Americans and blacks in thirty-eight states and forty-one countries around the world.

A majority of black leaders in the 1920s were preaching integration as a way of stemming the animosity and righting the inequality between the races. Garvey disagreed. He refused to support the assimilation policies of contemporaries like sociologist DuBois and union organizer A. Philip Randolph. Randolph, editor of the influential *Messenger* magazine, had arranged Garvey's first formal speaking engagement. Yet as the UNIA grew in popularity, Garvey rejected Randolph and other integrationists, labeling them weak. Many of his followers agreed. "Their approach to our problems was too doggoned tame!" says Garvey supporter Joseph

Bailey. "We needed to have that attitude of Marcus Garvey, that stand up on your feet and be ready to defend your manhood—at all times."[12]

Garvey challenged blacks to band together and fight back against oppression and the despicable Jim Crow laws of the South. This was new. Never before had a black leader so boldly called for people of color to stand up for themselves and take what was rightfully theirs. Even more shocking was Garvey's ambitious goal of creating an independent black nation, possibly in an African country. This would require blacks' complete economic and social separation from white America and a return to the roots and traditions once stripped from them. For many of Garvey's followers, the prospect of a return to the motherland was enormously exciting. Most blacks knew little about Africa, and what they did get—from newspapers and movies—was misleading. "Africa was called the 'Dark Continent,'" says Garvey supporter Charles Mills, "and the pictures we got of Africa in those days were cannibals running around in the jungles, puttin' people in pots. Garvey changed all that."[13] The UNIA's motto—"One God, One Aim, One Destiny"—encouraged blacks to unify around this common goal of return and renewal.

Most importantly, the UNIA was a movement of the masses, not an exclusionary club for intellectuals. It encouraged broad membership; any black person could join. The requirements included a fee of thirty-five cents, a photograph, and a signed pledge of support. In return African Americans from all walks of life— plumbers, bakers, sharecroppers, delivery boys, homemakers— were given something to believe in. They listened to their outspoken leader on the radio; read his newspaper, the *Negro World*; and marched with him in parades through Harlem or down Fifth Avenue, waving the red, black, and green flag of their nation in the making.

On parade days, many members even took to wearing a spiffy blue military-style uniform and hat, much like the kind worn by Garvey himself. As he rode through the city streets wearing his plumed commander's cap, Garvey waved to the large and cheering crowd—a black army hungry for his message of pride and self-reliance. He realized that spectacle and showmanship were essential ingredients in building a grassroots movement. Garvey

A supporter of Garvey stands outside the offices of the Garvey Club and the United Negro Improvement Association. Accusations of financial wrongdoings would bring Garvey and the UNIA down.

was a "master showman," says scholar Harvard Sitkoff, who "dramatized the . . . desperate necessity of change."[14]

Garvey carried his groundbreaking message of change from town to town and state to state, all across the country. It was a message that would one day serve as inspiration for the black arts movement. But in the early 1920s, white America could only watch in astonishment. "I am the equal of any white man," said

Garvey. "I want you [other blacks] to feel the same way."[15] Such rhetoric frightened white Americans, most of whom viewed the social order—with whites in control—as permanent.

At the height of his popularity, Garvey received many death threats from whites and harsh criticism from integrationist blacks. In 1922 one group, A. Philip Randolph's Friends of Negro Freedom, worked to undermine Garvey's hold on African Americans. But in the end it was accusations of more financial wrongdoing that led to Garvey's and the UNIA's downfall. Yet despite the movement's ultimate failure, "various large and influential activist nationalist groups generally descended from the Garvey movement,"[16] says historian James Edward Smethurst. In time Garvey's work became a touchstone for the artists and organizers who followed.

The Harlem Renaissance: A Look Within

Just as Marcus Garvey was pitching his message of black nationalism, young Missouri-born Langston Hughes was finding his poetic voice. Traveling by train to visit his father in Mexico, Hughes one day gazed out the window at the desert scenery rolling by and put pen to paper. He wrote of deep rivers, old rivers and connected them to the African American experience.

With the opening lines of his poem "A Negro Speaks of Rivers," Langston Hughes began his artistic journey. Although he was only nineteen when he wrote the poem, Hughes's distinctive, confident voice would soon help power the twentieth century's first major African American artistic movement.

In his poem Hughes blends a contemporary voice with the outlines of a rich and ancient African history—a history that predates slavery. For so long this unique and dignified collective past went unacknowledged or was forgotten by most Americans, black or white.

In time Hughes came to be known as the father of the Harlem Renaissance, an explosion of black artistic expression in the 1920s and 1930s. But Hughes only capitalized on a movement whose way was already paved by others.

Just after World War I, scholar James Weldon Johnson, encouraged by journalist H.L. Mencken, began calling for change for blacks. Johnson recognized that blacks had fought and died for the country, most recently in World War I, but they were still

Paul Laurence Dunbar: "Innate Artistic Talent"

In the shadow of emancipation, one son of former slaves, Paul Laurence Dunbar, began a unique artistic journey. Dunbar's first book of verse, *Oak and Ivy* in 1893, went virtually unnoticed, but his second, *Majors and Minors*, caught the interest of writer William Dean Howells. Later Howells called Dunbar the first black artist "to evince innate artistic talent." Although Dunbar died at the age of thirty-four, he produced six collections of poetry, four novels, and four volumes of stories. His work is characterized by his sharp eye for satire, as well as his use of African American dialect. His poem "The Mask" speaks of the dual roles a person of color was forced to play in a world made for and by white people.

Less than twenty years later, Dunbar's work would help fire the first genuine artistic movement of the new century.

Quoted in Paul Laurence Dunbar, *Black Voices: An Anthology of Afro-American Literature*. New York: Mentor, New American Library, 1968, p. 355.

given little respect. Despite Marcus Garvey's best efforts and his millions of followers, African Americans remained second-class citizens. For Johnson, racial inequality and injustice was a matter of mind-set. His solution was profound and revolutionary. "Nothing will do more to change this mental attitude and raise his [the black man's] status," he wrote, "than . . . through the production of literature and art."[17] There were not enough positive images of blacks, Johnson believed, and only through self-expression could such images be created.

The New Negro movement, as the Harlem Renaissance was then known, also embraced Africa itself. "Through much of the writing ran a spirit of optimism," says historian Robert J. Norrell, "that celebrated African Americans' survival of a harsh past on the African continent, and their expectation of better days ahead."[18]

But despite the call for optimism and a look homeward, in the summer of 1919 race riots broke out in a number of American

Paul Robeson: Looking Elsewhere for Equal Rights

For black artists and intellectuals in the 1920s, 1930s, and even 1940s, the American dream remained a dream deferred. The United States had yet to completely live up to the promise of its Constitution by ensuring African Americans equal rights and fair treatment. As a result many blacks looked to the Soviet Union as their last great hope for better jobs and more progressive political conditions. Famed singer and actor Paul Robeson was but one of the African American artists to travel behind the iron curtain for a closer look. In 1934, invited by filmmaker Sergei Eisenstein, Robeson received a lavish welcome across the Soviet Union. Less than ten years later, he became the target of an investigation by the FBI. Although he continued performing on stage, Robeson refused to appear in Hollywood movies because of their stereotyped portrayals of blacks. Despite his fight for equal rights and justice in the United States, Robeson's passport was revoked in 1950, and he was blacklisted in 1953 as a Communist. Robeson's career never recovered. He died in obscurity in 1976.

American singer Paul Robeson spoke in Russia in 1934. His passport was revoked in 1950 and he was blacklisted as a communist in 1953.

cities. The riots were sparked primarily by high unemployment and a lack of opportunities for those men returning from the war. Returning whites were angered because they now had to compete with blacks for jobs. During this "Red Summer," as it came to be known, whites attacked blacks in northern and southern cities alike, including Omaha, Nebraska; Washington, D.C.; Longview, Texas; and Chicago, Illinois.

Jamaican-born Claude McKay, like much of the country, read about the violent riots in the newspaper. He poured his emotions into a poem. He acknowledged that the death of black people might be inevitable. But, he wrote, the deaths would not be in vain if people died nobly and with convictions.

McKay's sonnet called the white murderers "monsters" and his poem ends with a call to self-defense.

McKay's black man was no weak, pathetic animal after all; he was strong enough to defend himself against the violence and the racism that had, for so long, troubled his people. McKay's poem was widely read as a call to arms. Forty-five years later, black artists heeded this call and took their struggle far beyond what McKay could have dreamed.

And while McKay's poem "If We Must Die" may have pushed open the door to black expression, it was the 1925 publication of the anthology *The New Negro*, edited by Alain Locke, that kicked the door in once and for all. Before long—and with the aid of white artists and patrons of the arts—black writers were being published in established, previously white-dominated magazines like the *Nation* and *Vanity Fair* and winning book contracts with major publishing firms.

One white supporter of the budding movement was Carl Van Vechten, a photographer and music critic who used his influence in New York City to bring together African American writers and powerful publishers. His 1926 novel *Nigger Heaven*, an enticing portrait of the Harlem nightlife, was labeled exploitation by some critics, including DuBois. Yet through his efforts and connections, Van Vechten was able to increase the nation's demand for the work of African Americans like Langston Hughes, Claude McKay, Jean Toomer, Countee Cullen, and Zora Neale Hurston.

As for the artists themselves, they determined to chart a new artistic course, one that rejected the history of European-influenced expression. It was, they insisted, time to stop imitating their former masters' works and begin celebrating the dignity and creativity brought to America's shores hundreds of years before.

In his famous essay "The Negro Artist and the Racial Mountain," Langston Hughes brushed aside the notion, held my many white Americans since the days of slavery, that the lives of African Americans were unworthy of art. He spoke for and to black artists of all types, as well as whites who might be suspicious of the power and potency of African American creativity:

> There is sufficient material to furnish a black artist with a lifetime of creative work. And when he chooses to touch on the relations between Negroes and whites in this country . . . there is an inexhaustible supply of themes at hand. To these the Negro artist can give his racial individuality, his heritage of rhythm and warmth, and his incongruous humor that so often, as in the blues, becomes ironic laughter mixed with tears. But let us look again at the mountain.[19]

The mountain, as Hughes saw it, was "this urge within the [black] race toward whiteness."[20] But instead of looking to whites, he suggested that black artists must look within. Hughes's essay became a rallying cry, a gauntlet thrown down not in anger but in confidence and certainty.

In the years to come, many in the black arts movement would sneer at the perceived foolishness of the Harlem Renaissance, a movement financially supported in large part by white patrons like Carl Van Vechten. Hughes and his contemporaries had not gone far enough in building a separate, distinct artistic vision, the critics would complain. Still, the Harlem Renaissance gave voice to the challenges facing African Americans and paved the way for the next steps along the road of social acceptance and change.

Civil Rights: A Nation of Voices

Despite the positive steps taken during the Harlem Renaissance, better days for American blacks were still a long way off. In his searing 1952 novel *Invisible Man*, Ralph Ellison, a novelist deeply influenced by the Harlem Renaissance, spoke for so many African Americans in the famous opening lines: "I am an invisible man. No, I am not a spook like those who haunted Edgar Allan Poe;

Zora Neale Hurston: Watching God

Perhaps the most significant female writer of the Harlem Renaissance was Eatonville, Florida, native Zora Neale Hurston. Born in Alabama but steeped in the dialect and traditions of Eatonville, Hurston studied anthropology at Barnard College with famed anthropologist Franz Boas. Her first book, *Mules and Men* (1935), is a collection of African American folklore and mythology. As her studies continued, Hurston became involved with the fledgling literary movement in Harlem. There she met Langston Hughes and other notable writers. Later Hurston traveled throughout the Caribbean collecting stories and studying the native peoples. Her best-known work, *Their Eyes Were Watching God* (1937), tells the story of light-skinned Janie Crawford. Janie is a tough and independent woman who suffers physical and emotional hardships before meeting Tea Cake, a younger man with whom she finds happiness.

By the 1950s Hurston's work had been virtually forgotten. Although Hurston continued to write, she never again got to see her work in wide circulation. Then, in the summer of 1973, writer Alice Walker searched for Hurston's grave, discovering it in an overgrown and forgotten segregated cemetery in Fort Pierce, Florida. Today Zora Neale Hurston is widely read and respected.

Zora Neale Hurston was one of the Harlem Renaissance's most significant writers.

nor am I one of your Hollywood-movie ectoplasms. I am a man of substance, of flesh and bone, fiber and liquids—and I might even be said to possess a mind. I am invisible, understand, simply because people refuse to see me."[21]

When not invisible, blacks suffered blatant racism. Despite the awareness and grudging respect given the black experience in the years following the Harlem Renaissance, the nation's laws remained essentially discriminatory and racist. But a legal transformation was on the horizon.

Encouraged and fought for by brave activists in the flowering civil rights movement, a 1954 Supreme Court decision broke with southern tradition and sent shock waves through the United States. *Brown v. Board of Education* made the integration of public schools mandatory across the country. Until then the law had required a "separate but equal" policy that in reality left most black schoolchildren with dilapidated schools and outdated textbooks.

In 1955 civil rights activist Rosa Parks refused to move to the back of the bus, a requirement for all southern African Americans at the time. Parks's calculated civil disobedience sparked the Montgomery, Alabama, bus boycott. The boycott lasted 381 days —more than a year—until the city's financially strapped bus company gave in: Blacks could sit anywhere they liked.

The boycott was led by a brash and outspoken young minister named Martin Luther King Jr. King's tactics of nonviolence, borrowed from Indian leader Mohandas Gandhi, struck a chord with white and black America. His triumphant speeches and writings inspired millions to follow his dream of integration, equality, and peace.

The seeds of black nationalism and the black arts movement sprouted at the same time as the civil rights movement. But it rejected the idea of integration and assimilation with white America. For black nationalists, King, despite his good intentions, was not the answer to their problems. He and his movement were too eager to negotiate with whites, they believed; negotiation was a sign of weakness, not strength. Black nationalists also called for a radical rethinking of the tactics used in fighting a system built by and for white Americans: they would not ask for change, they would demand it; they would no longer rely on whites for support and instead would support each other; and no longer could blacks reject violence, as King did. Too many of them had died at the hands of whites.

Often considered the antithesis of King, black nationalist leader Malcolm X made it plain: "Our enemy is the white man." Like Marcus Garvey forty years earlier, Malcolm X called for a separate nation, "a land of our own, where we can reform ourselves, lift up our moral standards, and try to be Godly."[22] The black arts movement aimed for such reform through words, music, and action, but it would do so without its fiery leader.

Chapter Two

The Rise of the Black Arts Movement

LeRoi Jones read the evening paper the night of February 21, 1965, and was shattered. His hero, Malcolm X, was dead, gunned down in cold blood in front of hundreds of people. Jones, a renowned thirty-one-year-old poet and playwright, read the accounts of the assassination over and over again.

The Audubon Ballroom, between Broadway and Saint Nicolas Avenue in Harlem, was used as a dance hall and for civic functions. Four hundred wooden chairs had been set up for the day's event. When Malcolm X's young assistant arrived at 1:30 P.M., she noticed at least four men had already taken their seats directly in front of the stage. She thought nothing of it; it was common for audience members to come early. Malcolm X was world famous, not only for his views on black nationalism but for the fiery nature of his speeches. The thin, bearded leader had the unique ability to captivate onlookers with his well-crafted words, his vocal power, and his dark, steely eyes.

Nearly half an hour later, the ballroom was nearly full. Despite the dangers, Malcolm X had rejected the idea of searching people at the door for weapons. "It makes people uncomfortable," he said. "If I can't be safe among my own kind, where can I be?"[23]

At almost two o'clock Malcolm X arrived and took a seat backstage. The man who was to introduce him, Rev. Galamison, was late. In his stead, Malcolm X sent his aide Benjamin X to speak to the excited crowd.

By 3:00 P.M. Galamison still had not shown, and Benjamin X introduced his mentor. Striding to the podium, Malcolm X looked confident. He offered the crowd the familiar Muslim greeting: "Asalaikum, brothers and sisters!" Some in the audience responded, "Asalaikum salaam!"[24]

Suddenly, a scuffle broke out in the crowd—people pushing and shoving; Malcolm X tried to calm them. "Let's cool it, brothers,"[25] he said. But the commotion distracted speaker and audience long enough for at least three gunmen to approach the

Followers tend to Malcom X as he lies mortally wounded on the stage of the Audubon Ballroom in Harlem after being shot on Febuary 21, 1965.

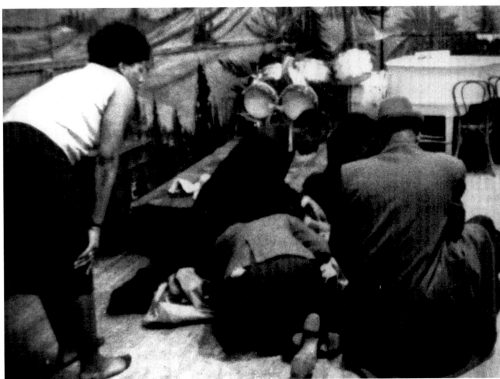

stage and begin firing. "Men, women, and children ran for cover," wrote reporter Stanley Scott. "I saw Malcolm hit with his hands still raised, then he fell back over the chairs behind him."[26]

LeRoi Jones Leads the Charge

To LeRoi Jones, the bullets that felled Malcolm X were the shots heard around the black world. Continued racial injustice and the murder of his idol convinced Jones that the time was right for a radical rethinking of the role of blacks in American society. In fact, he had already begun making his mark, not only as an activist for black nationalism, but as a poet and playwright.

In 1964 Jones electrified the New York theater world with his provocative one-act play, *Dutchman*. The play, set in a dingy New York City subway car, centered on a mild-mannered black man who is propositioned, abused, and then brutally stabbed by a white woman. Now, a year after the play's premiere, Jones was distraught and confused by the news of the day. In his autobiography, he echoed the feeling of helplessness so many blacks felt: "Malcolm's death had thrown people up in the air like coins in a huge hairy hand."[27]

The Newark, New Jersey–born activist spent his artistically formative years in Greenwich Village, in downtown Manhattan. There Jones had lived an integrated life. Long connected with the American beat movement led by Jack Kerouac, many of his friends and even his wife, Hettie, were white. But Jones, by his own account, could no longer relate to his white friends. He was seething with anger. During a speech at the Village Gate, a white woman stood up and asked Jones if whites could help blacks in some way. "You can help by dying," he told her. "You are a cancer. You can help the world's people with your death."[28]

The day after Malcolm X's assassination, Jones held a press conference in New York, announcing his plans to begin the Black Arts Repertory Theatre and School (BARTS). A month later, Jones arrived in Harlem to "help raise the race," moving into a brownstone on 130th Street. For generations Harlem had been the center of African American culture. Thus his relocation to Harlem marked a new beginning. He decided, he said, to jump "headlong back into what he [Jones] perceives as the blackest, native-est."[29] It was, for Jones, a return to the roots of African American art and experience—a continuation of where it all began.

Sun Will Come Out

LeRoi Jones, later known as Amiri Baraka, first met free-form musician Sun Ra and his Arkestra in Chicago in the early 1960s. The free-jazz musician made an impression on the young writer: "They put on weird clothes, space helmets, robes, flowing capes. They did rituals, played in rituals, evoked lost civilizations, used strangeness to teach us open feeling as intelligence," says Baraka. But most of all, Ra and his band played, borrowing from a wide range of sources, including Latin, Indian, Caribbean, and, of course, African. To these, Ra added electronics, unusual in jazz at the time. Steeped in African folklore, Ra's work expressed "communal consciousness," says Baraka. But the music was not for everyone. Some critics called it noisy and hard to bear; but for others it provided a propulsive soundtrack to the black arts revolution.

Amiri Baraka, "Sun Ra," *African American Review*, June 22, 1995.

Amiri Baraka, standing, founded the Black Arts Repertory Theatre in Febuary of 1965. He is shown here teaching an acting class.

Along with writer and friend Larry Neal, Jones forged a unique vision for the future of black culture. Neal told *Ebony* magazine that the black arts movement "seeks to link . . . art and politics in order to assist in the liberation of black people."[30] The new theater and school attracted African Americans from all over the East Coast. The theater held classes in poetry, playwriting, music, and painting. And as a sign of the black arts movement's growing influence—and perceived threat to white America—two FBI agents took a history course taught by Harold Cruse, author of *Crisis of the Negro Intellectual*. The agents apparently sought to better understand the growing movement and its potential danger to the white establishment.

Aside from community education, every Sunday Jones, Neal, and other artists organized free concerts, poetry readings, and art

Larry Neal: Black Arts Philosopher

———◼———

"Bringing art to the people, black art to black people, and getting paid for doing it was sweet," wrote LeRoi Jones/Amiri Baraka in his autobiography. But without Larry Neal, he acknowledges, that might not have been possible. Neal, born in Atlanta, Georgia, moved north and earned his degrees at historic Lincoln University in Pennsylvania in the early 1960s. Before long, though, Neal's writing on the importance of black art, in theater and elsewhere, became the touchstone for the black arts movement. In 1968 Neal, along with Jones, published *Black Fire*, an anthology of progressive black voices, including Sonia Sanchez, Kwame Ture, Harold Cruse, and Stanley Crouch. The book came to be seen as the philosophical foundation for the movement and propelled Neal into the role of resident theorist. He called, among other things, for the weeding out of white and European influences in the art of African Americans. This artistic separatism was, Neal insisted, the only sure way to create a pure black aesthetic. After the decline of the Black Arts Repertory Theatre, Neal taught at Yale and Wesleyan universities, as well as the City College of New York. He died in 1981.

Amiri Baraka, *The Autobiography of LeRoi Jones*. New York: Freundlich, 1984, p. 213.

shows. "We brought new music out in the streets, vacant lots, playgrounds, parks," wrote Jones in his autobiography. To make this happen, the theater created a jazzmobile. "We had trucks with stages we designed from banquet tables held together by clamps," said Jones. "And Pharoah, Albert, Sun Ra, Trane, Cecil Taylor, and many other of the newest of the new came up and blew."[31]

Despite its initial success, the theater and school soon ran into financial trouble. Much of the organization's funding came from a Harlem antipoverty agency with ties to the state and federal government. But its Afrocentric events and nationalistic goals made some white officials nervous, and the money dried up. This, along with internal struggles between its leaders, forced BARTS out of business. It lasted less than a year. But the experiment was not dead. In fact, it had just begun. Jones moved back to his hometown of Newark, helped found an arts organization named Spirit House, continued writing, and changed his name. He would be heard from again.

Black Theater Lives

In New York, the Black Arts Repertory Theatre was only one part of a growing, citywide explosion of black performances. The New Lafayette Theatre in Harlem, founded in 1967, staged the works of many up-and-coming playwrights, also providing work for African American actors, stage managers, lighting designers, and costumers.

Started by Robert Macbeth, the New Lafayette hired playwright Ed Bullins as its writer-in-residence. Hailing from the San Francisco Bay Area, Bullins's star began to rise nationally. His plays, including *We Righteous Bombers* and *Goin' a Buffalo* were confrontational and stark, painting a bleak portrait of the bigotry and economic inequity inherent in the United States. *Goin' a Buffalo* centers on a group of Los Angeles pimps and prostitutes who move east seeking a better life, only to find their dreams dashed. Bullins's bold work influenced the next generation of black playwrights, including Pulitzer Prize–winner August Wilson.

The New Lafayette, in time, was forced to move downtown after the theater was set on fire. Still, according to historian James Edward Smethurst, it became "a lightning rod for many of the intense debates"[32] over the direction of black art in New York City.

The National Black Theatre lasted longer and, like the New Lafayette, played an integral part in the growing influence of black performing arts. But founder Barbara Ann Teer looked beyond the world of theater by encouraging members to broaden their experience with African American customs by attending black churches and other traditionally African American cultural activities.

Dancers perform the first ballet at the Lafayette Theatre in Harlem on November 20, 1937.

Another long-standing organization with ties to the black arts movement is the New Federal Theatre. Led by director and writer Woodie King Jr., the New Federal exists today. It has a reputation of presenting work by well-respected writers of color, including Charles Fuller, author of the award-winning *A Soldier's Play*, about murder and racism on a southern military base.

King's vision extended to other cultures as well. His original idea was that the New Federal would provide a venue for not only black theater but for Asian, Jewish, and Latino presentations as well. Still, despite the inclusive nature of the New Federal, King remained adamant that "black plays should be directed by African American directors, Jewish plays by Jewish directors, and so on,"[33] says Smethurst. Who better to understand a race's unique experience and history, King believed, than a member of that race?

One black playwright who knew all too well the challenge of being black and female in America was Adrienne Kennedy. Born and raised in Pittsburgh, Pennsylvania, Kennedy took an interest in drama early on and soon moved east, to New York City. There, she studied with Pulitzer Prize winner Edward Albee and in 1964 wrote *Funnyhouse of a Negro*. In the play an African American woman named Sarah struggles with her identity and race. Sarah is torn by self-hate and alienation. Critics either praised the honesty and experimental form of the play or put it down as being confusing. Yet *Funnyhouse* won Kennedy a prestigious Obie Award and placed her at the forefront of young dramatists of the 1960s.

Black Arts Poetry: Language of the Struggle

From its inception, the black arts movement was dominated by strong male voices and visions. Women, like Adrienne Kennedy, while not exactly discouraged from participating, often found themselves in secondary roles.

All that began to change in the late 1960s. Poets Nikki Giovanni and Sonia Sanchez, in particular, helped broaden the perspective of the movement. Taking inspiration from jazz music, poems became jagged, elliptical, and apparently improvisational. The European conventions of verse were gone, replaced by open, streetwise tones steeped in the vernacular of the people. Poems voiced joy, sadness, pride, and outrage; but now, the voice was openly black, politically black.

Giovanni's early work was raw, outraged at the state of blackness in America. In her 1968 poem "The True Import of the Present Dialogue: Black vs. Negro," she prescribed a remedy, writing that "niggers" must be killed and replaced by black men. The difference, she suggested, was one of responsibility, engagement, and pride.

Sonia Sanchez's poem "blk/rhetoric" speaks of finding new heroes for African Americans, ones who will not simply use culture and greed as ways of making money.

The style of Sanchez's and Giovanni's work was influenced, too, by the oral traditions of black ancestors. During slavery, blacks' only connection to their African past was through stories passed along—mouth to mouth—from generation to generation. The new/old language used in poetry of the black arts was a look forward and a look back; it was crafted to be shouted or sung to an audience gathered for the sharing of ideas.

For Us, by Us: Black Publishing

Initially, New York City was the black arts hub, but in other parts of the country, too—small hamlets and big cities—black artists such as Sanchez and Giovanni were now finding their voices. At the same time, more outlets for black work were springing up, enabling these voices to reach the wider community.

Small publishers like Detroit's Broadside Press presented new poets in its pages, including Sanchez. Broadside's first book project, a 1969 tribute anthology called *For Malcolm*, exemplified founder Dudley Randall's mission: publishing inexpensive books that would appeal to a wide array of African American readers.

One contributor to *For Malcolm*, Haki Madhubuti, would soon become one of the best-selling poets in the country, with such volumes as *Black Pride* and *Don't Cry, Scream*. Yet it is perhaps Madhubuti's commitment to the black community that is of most lasting value. Third World Press, housed in Chicago and started by Madhubuti, Jewel C. Latimore, and Carolyn Rodgers, dedicated itself to publishing works by black power activists. Their mission was to "provide in-depth reflections of ourselves by ourselves."[34]

Madhubuti, born Don L. Lee in the Deep South, had a difficult upbringing. His mother was a prostitute, and his sister gave birth to her first child at the age of fourteen. There were few places

Poet Nikki Giovanni's works were influenced by the oral tradition of her black ancestors.

to turn for a young African American. "I grew up hating myself," he remembers. Confused and feeling alone, Madhubuti sought solace in books; Richard Wright's *Black Boy* had a profound impact. "Art essentially saved my life,"[35] Madhubuti says. For Madhubuti, art also brought a deeper awareness of his culture and history, which eventually convinced him to change his birth name.

During the days of slavery, masters forced Anglo-Saxon or biblical first names and their family surnames on their human property. During the time of the black arts movement, more people of color took on traditional African names. For example, Malcolm X started life as Malcolm Little in Omaha, Nebraska. Upon joining the Nation of Islam, he used "X" as a tribute to his illiterate, enslaved ancestors, most of whom scrawled the letter when signing documents. Malcolm X was also known by the Islamic name El-Hajj Malik el-Shabazz.

What was important is that some African Americans now chose their own names after centuries of being labeled by others. This act was an integral part of their self-determination. "People who are aware of their own cultural heritage," says Haki Madhubuti, "essentially have names that reflect their heritage."[36]

Madhubuti and Dudley Randall's book publishing, as well as many journals such as *Black Dialogue, Umbra, Black America, Liberator*, and *Soulbook* helped define the black arts movement, providing a forum for an ongoing artistic and intellectual dialogue about historical, cultural, and social issues related to the black experience.

Blacks Arts and the Community

If African Americans were to be self-sufficient and independent from the white world and reconnect with their own heritage, then "a main tenet of Black Power is the necessity for Black people to define the world in their own terms,"[37] wrote Larry Neal. The taking of African names was only one part of this fresh classification.

Also essential to this transformation of self was a deeper commitment to the community in which a person lived, worked, and raised a family. But for a race of people long subjugated and discriminated against by a powerful white society, such commitment was by no means a given.

Local leadership was necessary to jump-start this new vision and establish a more self-reliant community. "We need independent black institutions," says poet and publisher Haki Madhubuti, "self-sustaining institutions such as community centers, churches, and black-owned and operated businesses." Despite the many financial and organizational challenges, Madhubuti proved it could be done. From its inception, his Third World Press pledged "to give back to the community that I'm a part of. . . . Our responsibility was to change the conversation."[38] To this end, Third World Press created the Institute for Positive Education, which held lectures, ran a bookstore, and showed films.

Yet Third World's institute was only the beginning, as black communities throughout the United States built organizations, artistic and otherwise, for the promotion of African American values and ideas. In 1967 critic George Breitman recognized this local and national revolution in the making and wrote about the need for such black institutions in the article "In Defense of Black Power":

> Up to now the capitalist masters of this country have been able to control or contain the efforts of black people to liberate themselves. . . . The main reason why black Americans are not closer to their goal of freedom, justice and equality is that they have lacked a mass movement and a leadership truly independent of the ruling class, its ideology and its institutions.[39]

Breitman praised Malcolm X and his "fearless independence." He viewed the movement and Malcolm X as kindred spirits, and he described the movement's struggle against colonialism and the United States' undeclared war in Vietnam. Like Malcolm X, Breit-

The Line

Those blacks who rejected white supremacy and those who did not were noted in Malcolm X's description of the field Negro and the house Negro of slave times. The field Negro hated his oppressors; the house Negro put up with them. The field Negro planned his escape from the plantation, while the house Negro satisfied himself with the small freedoms and better food inside the master's home. According to Peniel E. Joseph, "Malcolm defined the black masses as contemporary Field Negroes: black people, like himself, who were catching hell every day." Such a devastating comparison also forced African Americans to take a cold, hard look at their own actions in relation to equality in the United States. Malcolm X had drawn a line in the sand and asked millions of blacks which side they stood on.

Peniel E. Joseph, *Waiting 'Til the Midnight Hour: A Narrative History of Black Power in America*. New York: Henry Holt, 2006, p. 91.

man neither recommended violence nor discouraged it. But, he wrote, the movement "spurns the straitjacket of 'nonviolence' and proclaims the right of self-defense."[40]

Art as a Mirror

By 1965 the straitjacket Breitman wrote about was ripped away. Unlike the Red Summer of 1919, the riots of 1965 were sparked by deep-seated frustration and anger on the part of African Americans. Cities such as Los Angeles and Watts in California witnessed all-out guerrilla warfare, fires, and looting.

African American artists, along with the rest of the nation, could only watch helplessly as the erupting violence took on a life of its own. Yet their writing would eventually reflect what they saw as they worked to turn the racial tensions into explosive poetry and drama.

The Watts riots, especially, became a symbol of the racial upheaval being felt everywhere in the mid-1960s. On August 11, 1965, highway patrol officer Lee Minikus pulled over Marquette Frye. Minikus suspected the black youth of being drunk. As Frye and his brother Ronald were questioned, a crowd gathered. Rocks and garbage were thrown at Minikus and the other officers who had arrived to lend support. Before long, Rena Frye, the boy's mother, arrived. In the scuffle that ensued, all three family members were arrested.

The arrests only ignited the tensions between police and Watts citizens, many of whom broke store windows, fired guns, and destroyed private property. The riots lasted for six days. In the end, the National Guard arrived to quell the unrest. Thirty-four people died during the unrest, twenty-eight of them black. Police arrested four thousand people. Nearly a thousand buildings were destroyed or damaged. Cost to the city and its taxpayers exceeded $40 million.

Interviewed in 2005, retired officer Minikus has no regrets. "I would do exactly what I did at that time,"[41] he says. In later years Minikus and Marquette Frye became friends.

Like Minikus, Watts resident Tommy Jacquette is convinced he did the right thing. Now in his sixties, Jacquette takes issue with those who call what happened in Watts a riot: "We call it a revolt," he says, "because it had a legitimate purpose. It was a re-

The Fire This Time: Art and Riots

While race riots exploded across the country in the middle and late 1960s, artists, black and white, used the chaos and violence to inspire their work. In April of 1968 Canadian folk singer Gordon Lightfoot released *Black Day in July*. The song, a meditation on the Detroit riots, was quickly banned on American radio. Radio stations "don't want to upset their listeners," said Lightfoot in an interview. "It's a housewife in the morning, you know, like let's give her something to make her happy. I give something that's going to make her think."[1]

A more recent work that takes part of its inspiration from the panic in Detroit is the 2002 novel *Middlesex* by Jeffrey Eugenides. Eugenides' haunting prose captures the fear and helplessness of a city in flames and under fire:

> Outside, they were at it again: the snipers. . . . Each night, the sinking sun, like a ring on a window shade, pulled night down over the neighborhood. From wherever the snipers disappeared to during the hot day, they returned. They took up their positions. From the windows of condemned hotels, from fire escapes and balconies, from behind cars jacked up in front yards, they extended the barrels of their assorted guns.[2]

1. Quoted in Canadian Broadcasting Corporation, "Lightfoot Banned in the U.S.A.," April 13, 1968. http://archives.cbc.ca.
2. Jeffrey Eugenides, *Middlesex*. New York: Picador, 2002, p. 243.

Police arrest a rioter as the Watts area Los Angeles, CA, burns from rioting in August of 1965.

sponse to police brutality and social exploitation of a community and of a people. . . . I think any time people stand up for their rights, it's worth it."[42]

Jacquette's ideas were echoed in the music and poetry of the time. In his poem "Black Art," LeRoi Jones argued for brutal, take-no-prisoners poetry that took on the police and licked them.

Chapter Three

Cultural Influences and Identity

In 1965 LeRoi Jones gave voice to the black artistic vision in his poetry and plays.

He and others associated with black arts sought to incorporate the whole of black experience into their work, including the connection to Africa itself.

This idea was not a new one. The philosophy of Pan-Africanism —espoused by many in the black arts movement—focuses not on the differences of the African peoples but on what unites them and promotes unity against governments worldwide that seek to oppress Africans. The term itself, coined in the early twentieth century, means "all Africanism."

Noted writer and sociologist W.E.B. DuBois has been called the father of Pan-Africanism. According to historian Manning Marable, DuBois's book *The Souls of Black Folk*, published in 1903, "helped create the intellectual argument for the black freedom struggle in the 20th century."[43] Pan-Africanism promoted resistance to imperialism, in which a dominating country overwhelmed a smaller, less powerful one. In the 1960s black arts would use similar language to describe white America's control of blacks.

African Influence: The 1966 World Festival of Negro Arts

Less than ten years before the black arts movement came to prominence, the push for a deeper understanding of Africa and its relation to people of color throughout the world gained new traction. In the late 1950s the Society of African Culture called for an arts summit. After much planning the World Festival of Negro Arts opened in the West African nation of Senegal in 1966. Considered the first of its kind, the festival showcased the work of black artists from all over the world. An exhibit of Nigerian art was held in the town hall of the capital city, Dakar. Senegalese painter Iba N'Diaye's canvases were presented, and a filmmaking prize was awarded to director Ousmane Sembène for the first full-length film by an African, *La Noire de*. Twenty-five hundred artists and twenty-five thousand attendees crowded the many venues. Honored guests included American composer and bandleader Duke Ellington and poet Langston Hughes. Organizers described the festival as a celebration of African culture, a culture whose impact was now being felt worldwide.

"It successfully showcased the very real achievements of blacks in the world of arts and letters," says scholar Tracy D. Snipe, "along with their unique contributions of jazz, blues . . . spirituals. . . . The festival provided an extraordinary venue for black artists to demonstrate their achievements before a world audience."[44]

The black arts movement, too, celebrated African culture. Black citizens throughout the country had begun dressing in traditional African clothing and using traditional African names. But despite an allegiance to their homeland, some African Americans—including many artists—were skeptical of the festival's purpose.

It was widely known that the U.S. government funded the festival. Black arts leaders viewed the 1966 Festival of Negro Arts as a way for President Lyndon B. Johnson to push his civil rights program—the Great Society—by portraying blacks as less threatening than many whites believed they were. One American diplomat said as much by claiming the festival helped demonstrate "that Negroes are genuine participants in the 'mainstream' of 20th century American life" and "to demonstrate the interest of the United States in Negro and African art."[45]

"Nothing but a Nigger"

■

In 1884 W.E.B. DuBois wanted desperately to attend Harvard University in his home state of Massachusetts, but his family could not afford the tuition. Instead, DuBois gained admission to Fisk College in Tennessee; this, his first trip to the South, was one he would never forget. Thereafter, he traveled throughout the world, speaking out against the ignorance of racism. In 1903 he published *The Souls of Black Folk*, in which he criticized rival Booker T. Washington for insisting it was too soon to insist on civil rights for blacks.

In subsequent years DuBois cofounded the National Association for the Advancement of Colored People (NAACP) and edited its *Crisis* magazine. His experiences convinced him that racial integration was impossible in the United States, a country he saw as consumed with power. In 1951, after calling for a ban on nuclear weapons and refusing to register with the government as a "foreign principal," DuBois was indicted. Although he was acquitted of any crime, DuBois left the United States for Ghana in 1961. There he renounced his American citizenship and joined the Communist Party. On his ninety-first birthday, DuBois said, "In my own country for nearly a century I have been nothing but a 'nigger.'"

Quoted in Chester J. Fontenot and Mary Alice Morgan et al., eds., *W.E.B. DuBois and Race*. Macon, GA: Mercer University Press, 2002, p. 168.

William E.B. DuBois published *The Souls of Black Folks* in 1903. He criticized Booker T. Washington for insisting that it was to soon to insist on Civil Rights for blacks.

Black arts writer Larry Neal remained unconvinced by the government's motives. Wrote Neal:

> Hundreds of artists of African descent came to what could have been a most significant event. Only, they found that it was constructed to attract everyone but Black people. The performances were attended by ninety-percent European and American whites; while the bulk of the Senegalese people either could not afford the festival, or were somehow discouraged from going.[46]

Fanon's *Wretched*: Fighting Colonialism

The World Festival of Negro Arts may have brought the plight of non-American blacks into sharper focus. And by now members of the black arts movement, especially, began speaking out against colonialism in the developing world, most notably in Africa. The continent was rife with examples of peoples of color dominated by European nations. The growing awareness of racism and subjugation throughout the world inspired black artists as never before.

In 1961 a study of colonialism sent shock waves through the black arts movement. *The Wretched of the Earth*, written by intellectual Frantz Fanon, was a call to arms. The cover of the 1968 edition of the book trumpets it as "The Handbook for the Black Revolution That Is Changing the Shape of the World."[47]

Early in the book Fanon compares the colonists' town with that belonging to the colonized people. In his description, the artists and intellectuals of the black arts movement recognized their own inner cities:

> The settlers' (colonists') town is a strongly built town, all made of stone and steel.
>
> It is a brightly lit town; the streets are covered with asphalt, and the garbage cans swallow all the leavings. . . . The settler's feet are protected by strong shoes although the streets of his town are clean and even, with no holes or stones.
>
> The Negro village is a place of ill fame, peopled by men of evil repute. . . . It is a world without spaciousness; men

live there on top of each other. . . . The native town is a hungry town, starved of bread, of meat, of shoes, of coal, of light. . . . It is a town of niggers and dirty Arabs.[48]

Fanon himself came from a middle-class family on the island nation of Martinique. His early life afforded him a front-row seat to

In 1961 Frantz Fanon published *The Wretched of the Earth*, a study of colonialism that sent shock waves through the Black Arts Movement.

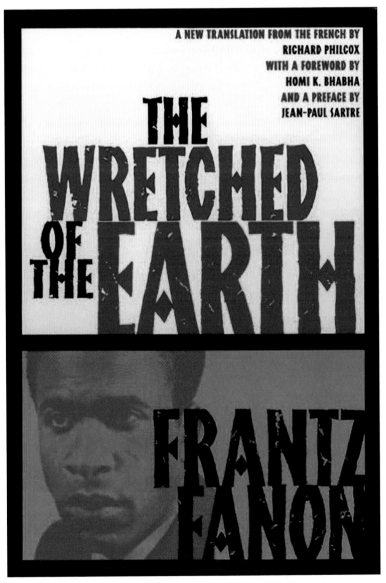

A NEW TRANSLATION FROM THE FRENCH BY
RICHARD PHILCOX
WITH A FOREWORD BY
HOMI K. BHABHA
AND A PREFACE BY
JEAN-PAUL SARTRE

THE WRETCHED OF THE EARTH

FRANTZ FANON

the hardship, poverty, and utter despair associated with colonialism. For centuries Great Britain and France had fought over his country. In 1925, the year of Fanon's birth, France controlled it.

During World War II Fanon had loyally fought to free France from Nazi control and remained there to study once the war ended. During these years, Fanon began writing down his thoughts on being a black intellectual in a white man's world. He became interested in the mental burdens put on the colonized person like himself by the ruling country. It was a confusing existence, he admitted. He considered himself French, but he found racism among white Frenchmen hard to accept. The lack of hope experienced by so many oppressed people was, Fanon believed, related to this sense of confusion and conflicted sense of loyalty.

Such ideas were only reinforced during Fanon's next call to action. In 1954 the North African nation of Algeria, also a colony of France, was rocked by civil war. French colonies were legally considered French soil. Algeria's native Arabs, led by the National Liberation Front (FLN), revolted against French rule. The vio-

Father of Fanon

■

Anticolonialist Frantz Fanon's conscience may first have been stoked by his teacher Aimé Césaire. Césaire, also born in Martinique, had been away for many years in Europe. While on a scholarship in Paris in the early 1930s, he met Léopold Sédar Senghor and Léon Damas. Together, the three young men founded a literary magazine called the *Black Student*, which marked the beginning of the negritude movement. Heavily influenced by the American Harlem Renaissance, the movement was outspoken on issues such as French colonialism and African identity.

Césaire, also a respected poet, returned to his homeland in 1937, where he taught Fanon at the Lycée Schoelcher. At about this time, Césaire turned his attention to the issue of Martinican identity. In the 1940s, as his reputation grew, he produced more poems, founded another literary journal, and in 1945 was elected to a post in the French National Assembly for Martinique. Since that time Césaire has continued speaking out against oppression. Martinique's international airport is now named for him.

lence of the uprising shocked many French citizens. Bombings resulting in mass casualties were carried out by the FLN on a regular basis. The French government retaliated with harsh measures, including the torture and execution of suspected rebels and the murder of innocents. Fanon moved to Algeria to aid the Arab rebels. During one incident he was severely wounded.

But Fanon lived long enough to propose a stark solution to the shameful crime of colonialism. In *The Wretched of the Earth*, he imagined a new world, one where the word *white* no longer signified good and *black* no longer signified evil, as in the past. This new world, he said, would come at a price: Only through violent revolution could it be achieved. "Violence is a cleansing force," he wrote. "It frees the native from his inferiority complex and from his despair and inaction; it makes him fearless and restores his self-respect."[49]

Fanon's ideas were deeply influenced by Marxism. Derived directly from the work of nineteenth-century German philosophers Karl Marx and Friedrich Engels, Marxism highlighted the contributions of the working people, called the proletariat. The Marxist idea that history is the story of class struggle—the powerful versus the subjugated and exploited—changed the thinking of many in the black arts movement.

Fanon's Marxist interests and support for the use of force gave voice to what so many in the black power and black arts movements strongly believed: The only way to achieve power was to take it. Writer Larry Neal echoed Fanon when he said, "The cultural values inherent in western history must be either radicalized or destroyed."[50]

In the coming years black arts reflected this push for armed revolution. Through poems, plays, and musical expression, artists demanded recognition of their struggle and their past; whites had no choice but to acknowledge both the pain and the beauty of the African American journey.

Free Jazz: Finding a Voice

The black arts movement required a new language to express itself. The old forms would no longer do. Harlem Renaissance writers had borrowed much of their form and style from the blues, but the younger generation needed a contemporary structure that would help convey its uniquely political and subversive image.

In 1963 LeRoi Jones published a revolutionary look at the roots of music in the United States. *Blues People: Negro Music in White America* remains a seminal study of the connection between a people and an art form. Jones's work traced the origins of black music. Along the way, the author made important discoveries. "As I began to get into the history of the music," Jones wrote, "I found that this was impossible without . . . getting deeper into the history of the people."[51]

By the time of his writing it was clear that the major beneficiaries of black music were whites. While the forms were African American, artists like Elvis Presley and Jerry Lee Lewis sold millions of records and made millions of dollars by bringing traditionally black music to the white masses.

Yet despite the co-opting of rock and roll, one form of American music remained steeped in the language of black culture: jazz. Like the moon, art shifts and works its way through many phases over time. In the late 1950s, as a new black consciousness was beginning to grow in cities across the country, jazz musicians looked for new ways to express the times. World War II had ended more than a decade before. Black artists would no longer be hemmed in by European forms of expression; neither were they completely satisfied with the bebop jazz musing of pioneers like Miles Davis, Charlie Parker, and Dizzy Gillespie.

Upon his arrival in New York City in 1959, alto saxophonist Ornette Coleman announced that jazz must be "free." For Coleman, this meant, according to historian Geoffrey C. Ward, "employing strange scales, filled with vocalized smears and cries, seemingly unrelated either to a recognizable theme or to anything going on around him."[52] Free jazz, also known as "new thing," confused many listeners, including other musicians, but Coleman was committed to breaking new ground and following his own musical muse. "The theme you play at the start of the number is the territory," he explained. "What comes after, which may have very little to do with it, is the adventure."[53]

Another jazz giant was saxophonist John Coltrane. Before superstardom, Coltrane had played with some of the best musicians of the time, including Miles Davis. But by 1962 Coltrane's own legend was being burnished. He was famously

Saxophonist John Coltrane performs on stage in 1962. He preferred that his music be a medium for changing hearts and souls.

Mother Gwendolyn

If the black arts movement had a matriarch, it may have been Gwendolyn Brooks. Born in Topeka, Kansas, in 1917, she spent the majority of her childhood in Chicago. After attending Wilson Junior College, Brooks became a homemaker and a poet. Her first book, *A Street in Bronzeville*, was published in 1945, twenty years before the black arts movement officially began. Despite this, her strong and sympathetic voice resonated with young writers. She experimented with language and wrote of gang life—life she had only observed from afar. Still, Brooks wrote with authenticity and understanding, and her words echoed the frustration of a whole generation. When black power came to prominence, she was ready for it. Writing poems about Malcolm X and encouraging younger writers to stand up for what they believed in, Gwendolyn Brooks set an example of strength and honor that the black arts movement deeply respected. She was the first African American awarded the Pulitzer Prize.

Poet Gwendolyn Brooks was the first African American to be awarded the Pulitzer Prize.

obsessive about his work. When his wife, Alice, was out, Coltrane could ignore the phone and knocks at the door. He was compulsive about playing, just as he had been about drugs and alcohol in years past.

In 1957 Coltrane had been fired from Miles Davis's group because of his erratic behavior and addictions. Dejected, Coltrane returned to his home in Philadelphia and one day decided to change his life. "I experienced," he later wrote, "by the grace of God, a spiritual awakening which was to lead me to a richer, fuller, more productive life."[54] Coltrane turned his life around and poured his newfound devotion into his instrument. In 1964 he recorded the album *A Love Supreme*, a sonic exploration of love for and faith in God. In writing about the work, Coltrane could have been speaking for many black artists who viewed their art as a force for change: "My music is my spiritual expression of what I am—my faith, my knowledge, my being. . . . When you begin to see the possibilities of music, you desire to do something really good for people, to help humanity free itself from its hang-ups. . . . I want to speak to their souls."[55]

While John Coltrane was never directly involved with the black arts movement, he was deeply engaged in the plight of African Americans. "John was very interested in the civil rights movement," said his wife, Alice. He deeply respected both Martin Luther King Jr. and Malcolm X. According to Alice, "He did see the unity in what they were trying to achieve . . . different approaches to the same goal."[56] Amiri Baraka puts it another way: "Malcolm told it like it was, and Trane played it like it was—hot and illuminating!"[57]

Yet Coltrane refused to become militant, instead preferring to use his music to change hearts and souls and uplift people. Still, Coltrane's record label, Impulse, recorded many musicians with a more politically charged approach, including Pharoah Sanders, Sun Ra, and Albert Ayler, all of whom had played many Sundays at the now-defunct Black Arts Repertory Theatre.

The music of the more militant members of the jazz community provided the soundtrack for the revolution and convinced more African Americans that a change was essential, even inevitable. But other black institutions would have to be transformed as well.

The Black Church Responds

African American artists and thinkers determined to alter the definition of what it meant to be black in America. To do this, old European-based images and beliefs had to be destroyed and white supremacy torn from its foundation, piece by piece. If the black arts movement used language, music, and images to reorder the world, then other black institutions were also intent on transformation.

For many African Americans, the church was the center of the community, the place people went for renewal and sanctuary. Yet in 1963, during the height of the civil rights movement, a Birmingham, Alabama, church was bombed, killing four little girls. This event—the senseless murder of innocents—riveted the nation. "I suddenly realized what it was to be black in America," said singer and pianist Nina Simone. "It came as a rush of fury, hatred, and determination. In church language, the Truth entered into me."[58]

What entered Albert Cleage in Detroit in the late 1960s was the realization that even the basic rituals and symbols of faith were steeped in tyranny and racism. Cleage, leader of the black theology movement, used his church as a proving ground for new ideas about what it meant to be a person of faith. His innovations became one more example of a cultural conversion that would have a profound impact on the way blacks viewed themselves.

First Cleage renamed his church the Shrine of the Black Madonna. Convinced that oppression and self-worth were linked, Cleage had traditionally white religious figures, including Jesus and his mother, Mary, painted with darker complexions. "White supremacy was so powerful," writes scholar Peniel E. Joseph, "that even the religious figures blacks looked to for eternal salvation were white."[59]

Cleage referred to contemporary religious practices as "slave Christianity" and worked to tie religion to the ongoing black revolution. "From the pulpit he cast Jesus as the Black Messiah," says Joseph. "Envisioning Jesus as a proud and radical black prophet who raged against political and economic oppression."[60]

Although Cleage was outspoken and militant on matters of white domination, he did not spare his own people. He spoke of "how good blacks were tearing things up"[61] but seemed unwilling to build communities and institutions.

Yet religion was not the only facet of life in which many blacks saw the heavy and dispiriting influence of whites. Before his death, Malcolm X had drawn a stark distinction between the "black revolution" and the "Negro revolution." The Negro revolution, embodied artistically in the Harlem Renaissance and politically in the civil rights movement of Martin Luther King, had made little progress for blacks, he said. Malcolm X continued: "Whoever heard of a revolution where they lock arms, as Rev. Cleage was pointing out beautifully, singing "We Shall Overcome"? You don't do that in a revolution. You don't do any singing, you're too busy swinging.[62]

Chapter Four

Assimilation or Self-Determination?

$\mathbf{A}$s the 1960s drew to a close, black leaders and citizens wrestled with the primary issue of their generation: Should they assimilate with white culture or walk the path of self-determination? The black power and black arts movements knew their answer. The murder of Martin Luther King on an April morning in Memphis, Tennessee, in 1968 was a tragic reminder of a brutal truth: Some whites would rather kill than accord blacks a place at America's table.

Three years after his death, Malcolm X's message of self-defense resonated with more African Americans than ever before; in short order, an organization based on his principles of black nationalism would rise. The black arts movement would play a vital role in taking that controversial message to the streets of America's big cities.

Art as Politics, Politics as Art

In 1967, less than two years after the Black Arts Repertory Theatre fell apart over a lack of funding and internal struggles, LeRoi Jones divorced his first wife and married poet Sylvia Johnson. Soon after, Jones also changed his name, a reflection, apparently, of his deeper commitment to black culture and his African ancestry. Taking the name Imamu (or spiritual leader) Amiri Baraka, the preeminent figure of the black arts movement served notice on white America. Although he would later drop "Imamu," Baraka remained a key figure in the movement, but now he was only one part of it.

Baraka's friend Larry Neal kept writing, too, becoming a bold voice and challenging old notions of black creativity and expression. "The Black Arts and the Black Power concepts both relate broadly to the Afro-American's desire for self-determination and

Novelist, essayist and poet Ismael Reed strongly criticized the black arts movement's ideas and methods.

nationhood," Neal wrote in his influential essay "The Black Arts Movement." "One is concerned with the relationship between art and politics; the other with the art of politics."[63] To Neal, politics was an art—one that had been used to control and subjugate blacks for generations. Was it not about time, he asked, that black artists and organizations took back the power of the image and the word to spread a new message and rally the masses?

Pride and a sense of self-worth were the essential qualities of the message. First blacks must recognize their own uniqueness and beauty, as well as their ties to a rich and proud culture. If the U.S. government ignored their urban communities, African Americans would not. Instead they would feed and educate their own people. In time blacks would even harness the power of the ballot box, electing representatives sympathetic to their needs.

These goals were lofty but not out of reach. But the system was broken. Black America needed a political vehicle for change, a group of men and women ready to lead it through the revolution. In 1968 the Black Panther Party was born. Through music and images the black arts movement helped fashion a potent new vision of black aggression and determination. Many members of black arts, including Larry Neal, even joined the Panthers and helped raise money for legal defense funds.

Yet not all black artists were as supportive of black arts and its politics. Poet and novelist Ishmael Reed was outspoken in his disdain for many elements of the black arts movement. Reed, controversial and left-wing like LeRoi Jones, had been a member of the radical Umbra Writers Workshop in the early 1960s. Umbra forged the artistic foundation of black arts through poetry readings and its namesake publication, and Reed's own work "affirmed various black cultures"[64] through the use of black folklore, according to author Jerry Gafio Watts.

Still, despite Reed's sympathy with many of the black arts movement's goals, he strongly criticized its ideas and methods, calling them a "goon squad aesthetic" and "tribalism for the birds."[65] For this, Reed found himself denigrated in the black press. Joe Goncalves, a strong supporter of the black arts movement and editor of the influential *Journal of Negro Poetry*, leveled harsh words at Reed, saying he was "always serving some white man's purpose."[66]

Such criticism only echoed the ongoing generational conflict developing between the older, more established black writers and this new group of intellectuals. For young Turks like Baraka and Neal, the Ralph Ellisons and Nathan Scotts of the black world were ancient history, unable or simply unwilling to take the necessary next steps toward self-reliance and power. As with so many new artistic movements—romanticism, naturalism, modernism—the previous school of thought was labeled obsolete and out of step. To gain a foothold, the new movement must destroy the old movement; from those ashes—and with the aid of new thinkers and new writers—a fresh aesthetic would rise and, perhaps, change things. This was the dream; the reality was far more complex.

Symbols of Power

The black arts movement evolved, in large part, in tandem with the African American political organizations of the time. One of the more influential political groups of the 1960s was the Student Nonviolent Coordinating Committee, or SNCC. First organized in Atlanta and Lowndes County, Alabama, in response to civil rights sit-ins in 1960, SNCC was persistent in its efforts to gain black voters equal rights, among other things.

Barely recognized as an organization at the time, it had a profound effect on civil rights and eventually attracted more radical members. What SNCC realized early on was that images could inspire and sometimes frighten people. They were the first group to choose the black panther as a symbol of the struggle, but they would not be the last. The black public needed powerful visions of blackness. The ferocious panther, crouching and ready to strike, fit the bill perfectly. In time the stealthy animal would adorn T-shirts, stickers, and banners across the country.

Such imagery was crucial, both for the black arts movement and for the communities it served because it drew a distinction between whites and blacks. "The Black Arts Movement presupposes a separate symbolism,"[67] said Larry Neal. Yet black nationalists also needed flesh-and-blood human beings to embody the strength and fortitude they believed necessary to achieve their goals.

SNCC organizer Stokely Carmichael was a panther personified. Beginning during his years at Howard University, Carmichael traveled to the Deep South to register black voters. Racist southerners

Hansberry's *Raisin*

Lorraine Hansberry's 1959 play *A Raisin in the Sun* took its title from a Langston Hughes poem. Centered on the Younger family, it takes place within the confines of a small apartment. There the family waits for a ten-thousand-dollar life insurance check to arrive. Once it does, mother Lena puts a down payment on a home in a white neighborhood so her grandson will have a better life. Family conflict ensues.

Unlike her main characters, playwright Hansberry grew up in a wealthy family, but she saw firsthand the difficult bargains African Americans were often asked to make in white America. Hansberry dreamed of creating characters that broke black stereotypes, not reinforced them. It took producer Philip Rose more than a year to raise the required funds for a Broadway run, but *Raisin*'s success was immediate, both critically and commercially. The play also drew a new audience to the Great White Way, or Broadway, as it is more commonly known. "Black people had not been attending the theater that much previously," said *Raisin*'s legendary director Lloyd Richards, "and here was a play that was about them."

Quoted in National Public Radio, "Present at the Creation: *A Raisin in the Sun*." March 11, 2002. www.npr.org.

Ruby Dee, left, Sydney Poitier and Diana Sands star in Lorraine Hansberry's *A Raisin in the Sun* on Broadway in 1954.

worked hard to keep African Americans from voting, but Carmichael and his SNCC coworkers often braved death to get people to the polls.

Although SNCC remained a nonviolent organization, Carmichael questioned the intelligence of that stand. "Well, I just don't see it as a way of life," he said, "I never have. But I also realize that no one in this country is asking the white community in the South to be nonviolent. And in a sense it is giving them a free license to go ahead and shoot us at will."[68] But the panther was only one symbol of black liberation. African Americans around the country were finding other ways to express their solidarity. Movie stars, musicians, singers, and even athletes began showing off their political sympathies. Another symbol was the raised fist. Printed on posters, record albums, and books, it represented unity, strength, and the willingness to fight for what one believed in.

At the 1968 Olympic Games in Mexico, star American runners Tommie Smith and John Carlos stoked controversy. Upon winning the gold and bronze medals respectively, Smith and Carlos bowed their heads and clenched and raised their black-gloved hands as the U.S. national anthem played. Smith wore a scarf around his neck, representing black pride, and both men wore black socks with no shoes as a show of support for impoverished American blacks. Their actions on the award stand landed them in deep trouble with the Olympic Committee, with a spokesperson calling the display "a deliberate and violent breach of the fundamental principles of the Olympic spirit."[69]

A year before the incident, Smith said black members of the Olympic team were considering a boycott of the games, but that never happened. Still, he said, "It is very discouraging to be in a team with white athletes. On the track you are Tommie Smith, the fastest man in the world, but once you're in the dressing rooms you are nothing more than a dirty Negro."[70]

The Panther Pounces

Olympian Tommie Smith grew up in the inner city and knew what life was like there. Part of the reality for blacks living in American inner cities in the 1960s was police harassment and brutality. Poverty and mass unemployment frustrated a generation of young black men and women. Some turned to crime. Crime brought increased police presence. As the mostly white police officers patrolled the predominantly black neighborhoods of Harlem or West Philadelphia or Oakland, tensions rose. The racism and misunderstanding that led to the riots in Watts and Detroit prevailed. Blacks viewed law enforcement as a major part of the problem; law enforcement was stretched to the limit and quick to judge. This made for a lethal mix.

In 1966 two young men from Oakland, California, former actor Bobby Seale and Huey Newton, formed the Black Panther Party for Self-Defense. Their initial goal was to watch closely the actions of police in their neighborhoods, but in short order their ambitions grew. Toting law books and machine guns, the Panthers called for armed revolution. Former SNCC chair Stokely Carmichael joined the party, too, saying, "If we don't get justice we're going to tear this country apart."[71] But these were no paper Panthers; their angry rhetoric was matched by violent action: In two years of open conflict, nine police officers were killed and fifty-six were wounded. Ten Panthers were killed. As far as the Black Panthers were concerned, only armed confrontation with those in power would help them attain their goals of separatism and justice.

The Black Panthers look matched their resolve. Typically dressed in leather jackets and sporting black berets and dark glasses, the Panthers' militant look outraged some and excited others. For many, though, it was the attitude that accompanied the image that captivated. "The thing that I really loved about the Black Panthers is that they refused to be ignored,"[72] says Father George Clements, a supporter.

Numerous black artists also supported the Panthers and their tactics. Writer Larry Neal joined one branch of the group. Amiri Baraka spoke at rallies and allied himself with their politics. His poetry had long reflected the aggressive rhetoric the Panthers now used to speak to their audiences.

The black arts movement virtually became a mouthpiece for the belligerent views and revolutionary spirit of the Black Panthers. Yet there were key differences, according to critic Mike Sell: "While the Panthers attempted to seduce and exploit the media by outrageous, blatant displays of hyper-masculine 'Blackness,' the Black Arts Movement sought to evade the white media [and

Huey Newton, right, the founder of the Black Panther Party, sits with fellow Panther Bobby Seale at party headquarters in 1967.

white traditions] by taking their revolutionary [ideas] to historically African American colleges and urban . . . African American communities."[73] Furthermore, says Sell, "While the Panthers saw the benefits of art primarily as a means to an end [such as fund-raising], Black Artists viewed art—as they viewed African Americans themselves—as both the means and the end of the revolution."[74]

Regardless of their differences, the two groups are linked because of their basic belief in black nationalism. Yet not all African Americans approved of the Panthers' tactics, or do today. "I question the whole purpose of the Black Panther Party," says former defender William O'Neal. "They were necessary as a shock treatment for white America to see black men running around with guns just like black men saw the white man running around with guns. Yeah, that was a shock treatment.

Soul on Ice: Sexism or Symptom?

Eldridge Cleaver's 1968 book *Soul on Ice* was a popular and critical success. Cleaver's no-holds-barred attack on white America and even on fellow black writers such as James Baldwin stirred the nation. Cleaver began writing the book in prison in 1957, after being convicted on an assault charge. Upon his release in 1966, his star rose, first as a proud Black Panther and then as a cultural critic. White intellectuals in particular hailed Cleaver's ideas as revolutionary and earth-shattering. To them, Cleaver was simply what he claimed to be: a victim of American colonialism. Even the violent behavior he bragged about, including the raping of black and white women, was seen as a symptom of white oppression. At least one critic, Bell Hooks, believes the wide support of Cleaver's book (and implicitly the behavior he writes about) has a clear explanation: "It is as though patriarchal white men decided that they could make use of militant black male sexism, letting it be the first and loudest voice of anti-feminist backlash." For Hooks, Cleaver's ideas were used to justify white men's fears of female equality.

Bell Hooks, *We Real Cool: Black Men and Masculinity.* New York: Routledge, 2004, p. 52.

Black Panther Eldridge Cleaver's book, *Soul on Ice*, was viewed as an attack on white America and fellow black writers.

It was good in that extent. But it got a lot of black people hurt."[75] As for whites, the Panthers "symbolized . . . the worsening threat of black violence in the United States," according to scholar Robert J. Norrell. "Whites generally perceived it as a direct challenge to law and order—and thus to their own security."[76]

Panther leader Huey Newton defended his party and his criticism of the police. In at least one case, he framed the argument in almost artistic terms. "I knew the images had to be changed," he said. "I know . . . that words, the power of the word, words stigmatize people and we felt the police needed the label, a label other than that fear image that they carried in the community."[77] The word now used by the Panthers to identify the police would stick: pigs.

Forging a New History: Black Studies in San Francisco

Times were changing. On the streets, in churches, at public events, African Americans were forcing Americans to take them seriously. After all, their dreams were American dreams. Yet for so many years they were denied a place at America's table.

Like many cities across the nation, San Francisco—across the bay from Oakland, the Black Panthers' hometown—was a hotbed of black power activity. Panther Eldridge Cleaver, recently paroled from prison, took command of the organization after Huey Newton and Bobby Seale were jailed for their activities.

Aside from his abilities as a leader, Cleaver was also a gifted writer, whose most famous book, *Soul on Ice,* became a best seller, selling more than a million copies. His work attracted many fans, including pioneering writer James Baldwin. Before the publication of his book, Cleaver had remained anonymous because of his past legal troubles; afterward, he became an instant celebrity and de facto voice for the movement, at least for a time.

Cleaver got people's attention, as did San Francisco's Black House, which became the center of West Coast black cultural nationalism. Playwright and poet Marvin X, formerly Marvin Jackmon, founded the organization with playwright Ed Bullins. Marvin X, connected for a time to the Black Muslims, or the Nation of Islam, is best known for his play *Flowers for the Trash-Man.* The drama chronicles the struggles of a black intellectual in an educational system designed for whites.

Black House itself "doubled as [Eldridge] Cleaver's primary residence [and] buzzed with activity," says writer Peniel E. Joseph, "welcoming artists, authors, and political activists."[78] Some of the artists and writers connected with Black House, many born in other parts of the country, stayed a while. LeRoi Jones and Sonia Sanchez did. The center of the revolution had switched coasts by 1968, especially after San Francisco State University took a bold step forward. The institution's Black Student Union voted to support a black studies program. This was the first time that such an educational program had been deemed acceptable by the academic elites.

But acceptance did not come immediately. In fact, San Francisco State administration condemned the program as "an intellectual and political fraud,"[79] according to Joseph. Only through the intervention and teaching of Jones, Sanchez, and Black Nationalist poet Ronald Snellings did the black studies program gain a foothold.

Regardless of the initial success, black studies and the African American students who supported it with Black Panther–style tactics often ran into trouble with the conservative university administration. But the fuse had been lit, and soon enough other campuses around the country were heeding the call. Black studies programs—some legitimate and some less so—sprang up almost everywhere.

Black artists led the charge, mingling with Black Panthers at rallies and writing poems of racial militancy. The Panthers and the poets were unifying as never before. According to Peniel E. Joseph, it was at this time that LeRoi Jones (the future Amiri Baraka) was transformed. "In front of three hundred students and numerous television cameras," writes Joseph, "Jones argued that the time had come for blacks to arm themselves."[80]

And arm themselves they did, with strong words and a willingness to push back. Author Henry Louis Gates remembers the electricity coursing through the lecture halls of many major universities, including one on which he saw poet Nikki Giovanni give a reading. "Her words seemed incandescent with racial rage," he says, "and each poem was greeted with a black salute. 'Right on! Right on!' we shouted, in the deepest voices we could man-

Dr. Nathan Hare:
Black Studies Pioneer

While growing up in segregated Slick, Oklahoma, in 1933, Nathan Hare's ambition was to become a boxer. Although Hare would return to this passion in later years, the fighting spirit of his youth served him well throughout his entire life.

Hare's academic career began at historically black Howard University in 1961, where his students included activist Stokely Carmichael. In 1966, after criticizing Howard president James Nabrit for insisting that Howard's student body should be 60 percent white by 1970, Hare was fired. Two years later, San Francisco State University hired Hare to develop an ethnic studies program.

Beginning with the premise that academia was, by nature, biased toward the history and experiences of Caucasians, Hare and San Francisco State students composed "The Black University Manifesto." The document called for an overthrow of black colleges based on white ideals—clearly a reference to Hare's former employer. In 1968 San Francisco State University became the first academic institution in the country to have a black studies department. Other important work followed, including Hare's

founding of the *Black Scholar*, the most important black journal since the *Crisis*. One of Hare's primary goals, he wrote, was "to build in black youth a sense of pride."

Quoted in William L. Van Deburg, *Black Nationalism: From Marcus Garvey to Louis Farrakhan*. New York: New York University Press, 1996, p. 160.

Dr. Nathan Hare headed up the nation's first Black Studies department at San Francisco State University in 1968.

age, each time Giovanni made another grand claim about the blackness of blackness."[81]

The righteous enthusiasm of Gates and other students throughout the nation ensured that black studies programs continued to flourish. They remain a vital part of the educational system at many colleges and universities today. The excitement and militancy such programs inspired in the late 1960s brought the ideas of the black power movement to cities and neighborhoods. And it was through the growth of communities, said the Reverend Al Cleage, that their goals would be achieved:

> Black people are not worried about white people in the suburbs. What we're trying to do is to control our own community, build our own black community and make it beautiful. Self-determination as a concept for black people is a part of the rebellion. It's a black revolution sweeping America and self-determination is the expression. That's what we want, that's what we're rebelling for. Oppression doesn't destroy people. The acceptance of oppression destroys any people.[82]

The black arts movement aided the larger movement by giving voice to the frustration, anger, and determination of an entire generation of young people. "There was a positive overall effect of the Black Arts concept that still remains," says Amiri Baraka. "We showed that we had heard and understood Malcolm and that we were trying to create an art that would be a weapon in the Black Liberation Movement."[83]

Chapter Five

Black Arts Hit the Mainstream

The black arts movement began underground—in people's homes, in corner cafes, and in university quads. Those in the know spread the word, attended cultural events, and even added their voices to the surging sense of empowerment. But in time what began as a radical fringe grew in stature and acceptance. It was cool to have soul. Once black arts and black artists were discovered by mainstream America, everything changed. African Americans gained a grudging respect, but first, they worked on gaining self-respect.

Black Is Beautiful

For centuries the image of American blacks was defined by white society. The beauty queens and movie stars splashed across newspaper front pages and TV screens were, with few exceptions, white. The blond hair and blue eyes that defined the all-American vision of perfection was as much a part of the culture as Mom's apple pie cooling on the windowsill. Thus the message to African Americans was that their typical features—wider noses, thicker lips—were ugly and less than wholesome. The psychological effect of such messages was stark: "Can you really imagine whole generations living and dying and never once having loved themselves,"[84] says poet Sonia Sanchez. Many could.

During the heyday of the black arts movement, poems, plays, and paintings began depicting African Americans as vibrant, strong, and beautiful. Despite the popularity and political relevance of the term, *black* was a misnomer. People of color came in all shades—some lighter, others darker. As for hair, the younger generation relinquished the close-cropped "do" or the lye-straightened conk of the past generation and grew their hair out into bushlike Afros. Many also took to wearing patterned dashikis and brightly patterned African shirts, blouses, and robes.

White Americans, as well as many blacks, viewed these developments as a serious threat to their way of life. After all, African Americans were already immersed in white society, often competing with whites for jobs and other essential benefits. There was no place, it appeared, for nonconformity.

Famously, all-black Howard University found itself on the front line of the debate. In the early 1960s Howard remained steeped in the integrationist past. This "Black Harvard" was conservative by the standards of the black power movement because its leaders felt it had to be to compete with its white counterparts. Generations of black doctors, lawyers, and other professionals received stellar educations at Howard; yet the question remained: Was Howard willing to step into the future, or would it wallow in its proud, but old-school, traditions?

Although black power had been holding rallies around the country, Howard's administrators and many of its students seemed reluctant to join the bandwagon. "As a student leader, you felt like you were being pulled apart," says Howard alumnus Fred Black, "pulled in different directions by what you thought the right way to deal with the problem."[85]

In October 1966 five young women vied for the title of homecoming queen; only one of them, Robin Gregory, wore an Afro. "I felt it was real important at that time," Gregory says, "because the Black Power Movement was new, that we as people begin to accept ourselves, you know, just as who we were."[86]

Gregory and the five other women campaigned for two weeks for the title of homecoming queen. On the night of the announcement, as the stage lights dimmed in the auditorium, the audience waited with bated breath. Slowly, the revolving stage turned and the light rose. Former Howard student Paula Giddings remembers: "You saw the silhouette of her afro before you saw her . . . the auditorium exploded and everybody exploded."[87] Robin Gregory's crowning as queen marked a sea change for Howard University and for the country at large. Not only could black be beautiful, but students with the style and politics of black power were leaving their mark.

Actress Pam Grier was a star in blaxploitation films in the 70's and was the "poster child" for the Black Is Beautiful movement.

"That's what we tried to change when we moved into the black arts, black culture, black consciousness movements," says Sonia Sanchez. "I said never again will I allow anyone to live and walk on the planet earth and not like what they are, what they've been."[88]

Soul or No Soul

It is difficult to determine just who first used the word *soul* to describe a state of being. Jazz singer Billie Holiday had soul. Her voice was a bruised peach, an open sore. Holiday's rasp spoke of the drugs and alcohol she had abused; it also contained a road map to her life, written in the lyrics of great composers like George Gershwin and Johnny Mercer.

Legendary singer Sam Cooke sang soul, but he also *had* soul. A generation after Holiday's heyday, Cooke's 1965 ballad "A Change Is Gonna Come" was of the moment and ancient at the same time—the musical equivalent of Hughes's "A Negro Speaks of Rivers" decades before. The speaker is born near a river, and he, like the river itself, spends his life running. The song is melancholy but hopeful: someday things will change.

Despite its connection to the past, soul seemed contemporary and new. It attested to what African Americans wore, how they walked, and the language they used to speak to one another. "To be soulful," wrote Amiri Baraka, "is to be in touch with the truth and to be able to express it, openly and naturally and without the shallow artifice of commerce."[89]

Soul implied depth of spirit, a connection to what was uniquely hip and black. It was, says writer William L. Van Deburg, "essential to an understanding of the culture of Black Power. . . . If there was beauty and emotion in blackness, soul made it so. Soul was sass—a type of primal spiritual energy and passionate joy."[90] But one was not necessarily born with soul. Only those whose black consciousness had been raised had it. It implied a belief in the movement and a belief in the self.

Inevitably, as a greater sense of identity arose, black people began looking at each other with a critical eye. What you wore, what you ate, what you listened to, and what your politics were defined your state of "blackness." Were you "down," or were you "bourgie"? This question drew a line in the proverbial sand. *Down*

Singer Sam Cooke became the first soul singer with his 1965 hit "A Change is Gonna to Come."

suggested hipness, while *bourgie*, derived from the Marxist reference *bourgeoisie*, marked a person as arrogant.

Within the black community itself, competition was fierce, as some blacks tried to "outblack" one another. Such infighting proved that self-definition is as much of a challenge as definition by others.

Pop Music and a Wider Audience

The black arts were never a secret. Baraka and other artists promoted their ideas and ideals loudly and frequently. Yet the intense politics and radical tactics were too militant, too angry, for some in the general public. Pop music, on the other hand, was broadly accepted.

Berry Gordy's Motown Records transformed the Motor City of Detroit into Hitsville, U.S.A. Accomplished recording artists like Diana Ross and the Supremes, Smokey Robinson and the Miracles, and the Temptations put soul music on everyone's radar and radio dials. But while the earliest Motown releases spoke of innocent love or the loss of it, ideas first voiced by the black arts movement began catching on with race-conscious songwriters and performers. "Baraka's 1966 call for politically conscious lyrics based on black protest proved to be the tip of a sizable iceberg," writes Peniel E. Joseph. "Fueled by the dual impulses of profit and politics, black recording artists helped propel Black Power into American popular culture."[91]

In 1966 singer Stevie Wonder recorded folksinger Bob Dylan's "Blowin' in the Wind." This was the first example of a popular black artist recording a song that reflected the true tenor of the times. Wonder's 1973 album *Innervisions* included an attack on disgraced president Richard Nixon as well as the long and plaintive "Living for the City," a story-song about a southern black family whose son travels to New York City and is arrested and jailed for a crime he did not commit. Wonder's work would continue to be suffused with black arts consciousness.

Spoken word poet Gil Scott-Heron confronted politics even more directly in 1970. Aggressively speaking over an African drum beat, Scott-Heron aimed to rile black Americans enough to get them out into the streets and participate because, he said, "The Revolution Will Not Be Televised."[92] Scott-Heron's producer, Bob Thiele, recorded mostly jazz musicians, including Coltrane, but Thiele clearly saw Scott-Heron's power as a politically progressive artist. According to historian Mark Anthony Neal, Scott-Heron and Wonder "had a significant impact . . . while functioning in very traditional roles as artists in tune with the social, cultural, and political imagination of the larger African-American community."[93]

The next year, in 1971, Motown star Marvin Gaye was primed to make a statement. After the death of his singing partner, Tammi Terrell, Gaye had considered retiring from the music business. That is until Four Tops singer Renaldo Benson brought Gaye an idea for a new song—a song about black America's confusing and painful present. Gaye, Benson, and songwriter Al Cleveland's collaboration yielded "What's Going On." The tune begins with the jovial sounds of black men gathering and greeting one another. After a moment, an alto saxophone snakes its way over an echoing drum beat. While the song is antiwar in its sentiments, Gaye could be speaking about the Vietnam War or the race war raging on America's streets, or both. "What's Going On" makes a stark case for understanding and healing, a far cry from the sometimes brutal rhetoric of the black power and black arts movements. While some social critics at the time may have considered Gaye's

Curtis Says "Think"

◼

Superfly may have been a throwaway for film critics (although an $11 million hit with audiences), but the soundtrack to the movie was anything but. Guitarist and songwriter Curtis Mayfield and his trio, the Impressions, had addressed social issues in past songs like "People Get Ready" and "Keep on Pushing." Combining his childhood churchgoing experiences in Chicago with an abiding awareness of the civil rights movement, Mayfield's work was always bold and became even more so after leaving the Impressions in 1970. In 1972 he composed the soundtrack for *Superfly*; it would serve as his greatest legacy. Although the movie's main character, Priest, was a drug dealer, Mayfield's soundtrack offered something far more inspiring: driving funk rhythms wed to intelligent and politically charged but positive lyrics. Mayfield "ignored the movie's glorification of drug-dealing and hustling," says rock historian Nathan Brackett, "and instead painted an unflinching portrait of real people who get caught up in street life." Songs included the title track as well as "Freddie's Dead," "Pusherman," and the lush, meditative instrumental "Think." Mayfield's classic soundtrack gave black and white America much to think about.

Nathan Brackett, *The New Rolling Stone Album Guide*. New York: Simon & Schuster, 2004, p. 524.

message of unity naive, in 2004 *Rolling Stone* magazine voted it the fourth-greatest song of all time.

"Black popular music provided a sonic backdrop to the efforts of the new militancy," writes Jeffrey O.G. Ogbar. "For black nationalists, the old negro spirituals were antiquated rituals of a more passive . . . struggle."[94] Other politically conscious artists such as War, James Brown, and Edwin Starr also apparently spoke for writers like Baraka, who continued calling for "an art that would reach the people, that would take them higher, ready them for war and victory, as popular as the Impressions or the Miracles or Marvin Gaye."[95]

But this dream of a more politically driven art never became a complete reality. Popular culture outstripped any interest in the

Women's Work:
Maya Angelou and Lucille Clifton

Despite their relatively low profile during the black arts movement, female writers began lighting a new "black fire" in the mid to late 1970s. Maya Angelou, born in 1928 in Missouri, worked as a dancer, singer, and actor. In the early 1960s she met Martin Luther King and later became close friends with Malcolm X. Her first published work, *I Know Why the Caged Bird Sings*, was released in 1969. This autobiography chronicles the first seventeen years of Angelou's life, including her rape by her mother's boyfriend, after which Angelou did not speak for five years. Angelou has since published plays and poems, winning a Pulitzer Prize in 1971.

Lucille Clifton was raised modestly in Depew, New York. Neither of her parents had a formal education, but they inspired Clifton to read by buying her books. In her twenties, Clifton developed a minimalist style of poetry, meaning she used few words to express herself. Her brand of free verse often concentrates on the body, as in her most famous poem "Homage to My Hips."

Like Angelou, Clifton's work is uniquely feminine and strong. Her honors include serving as Maryland's poet laureate and two grants from the National Endowment for the Arts.

Quoted in Patrice Vecchione, ed., *The Body Eclectic: An Anthology of Poems*. New York: Holt, 2002, p. 65.

more radical political tactics of the black arts movement. Music would remain an essential tool for continuing the struggle, long after the black arts movement had officially passed into history.

Blaxploitation

Another popular art form ripe for African American influence was film. The cinematic images of African Americans had changed little over the years. From the age of Edison's celluloid experiments in the late 1800s to the Hollywood studio films of the 1940s and 1950s, blacks were rarely portrayed on screen. When they were, white scriptwriters placed them in secondary roles, as butlers, maids, and chauffeurs. Black writers were occasionally hired, as Langston Hughes was to write the film *Way Down South* in 1939, but the final results often played like watered-down or white versions of the black experience. One exception, Oscar Micheaux's all-black *The Homesteader* in 1919, did not receive wide release. Yet Micheaux dreamed of a day when it would be different: "I'm tired of hearing about the Negro in an inferior position in society. I want to see them in dignified roles. . . . Also, I want to see the white man and the white woman as villains. . . . I want to see the Negro pictured in books just like he lives."[96]

Some strides were made early on. Kansas native Hattie McDaniel won a Best Supporting Actress Oscar for her role as Mammy in 1939's blockbuster *Gone with the Wind*. Paul Robeson, a civil rights activist, singer, and actor, made waves as much for his politics as for his memorable rendition of "Ol' Man River" from the musical film *Showboat*.

Even more controversial than Robeson, at least in film terms, was Stepin Fetchit, who became a comic performer as a teenager, performing in the popular minstrel shows of the early twentieth century. There he performed, sometimes in blackface makeup, as a slow-witted and lazy "coon." Eventually, Fetchit brought his act, offensive to so many African Americans, to the silver screen and commanded a large salary.

Yet even before the black arts movement seeped into the public consciousness in the 1960s, Hollywood studios sought to cash in with people of color without alienating their white audiences. Actors such as the debonair Sidney Poitier and the comic Bill Cosby represented Hollywood's mainstream version of black America

—smart, tough, yet acceptable to whites. Despite this cinematic change, the reality for many black Americans, especially those living in America's inner cities, was still not reflected in their local movie houses.

While the big studios were grappling with the subject of race on film, independent filmmaker Melvin Van Peebles had his own ideas. In 1970 he released *Watermelon Man*, about a white racist who wakes up in the body of a black man. While the film's popularity quickly attracted the eyes of Hollywood executives, they shunned his next movie, *Sweet Sweetback's Baadasssss Song*. Black audiences did not. Van Peebles is seen today as the father of blaxploitation cinema. The word combines *blax*, a slang version of *black*, and *ploitation*, an abbreviated version of exploitation. The implication—and often the reality—suggested the use of stereotypes, or broad, insulting portrayals of both African Americans and whites. Yet young and hungry filmmakers were intent on shattering the old image of blacks in film on their terms.

In 1971 noted photographer Gordon Parks agreed to direct *Shaft*, a studio-financed detective drama with a major difference: The cop was black, and so were many of the criminals. Starring Richard Roundtree, the film presented a tough-talking, lady-killing tough guy. Director Parks, though, remained uneasy about the genre his film was placed in. "I never associated *Shaft* with black exploitation. . . . Why is having a black hero who for the first time stood up for what he believed and fought the system . . . why call it an exploitation film?"[97] Historian Donald Bogle agrees, saying that *Shaft* "essentially was a white detective tale enlivened by a black sensibility."[98] Notably, the Oscar-winning title song by Isaac Hayes was a crossover blockbuster and went to the top of the pop charts.

In 1972 Parks's son, Gordon Jr., directed *Superfly*. The film's hero was no John Shaft, however. Instead, Priest (played by Ron O'Neal) dealt cocaine and violently battled his enemies. The film was a huge success, earning $11 million in its first two months of release. Although it traded on black and white stereotypes like so many other such films, Hollywood finally became virtually color blind: The only color it saw now was green.

Over the next ten years, hundreds of blaxploitation pictures were produced. Titles included *Black Belt Jones, Boss Nigger,*

Director/writer Melvin Van Peebles is seen today as the father of blaxploitation cinema.

Dolemite, and *Foxy Brown*, starring the gorgeous, Afro-wearing Pam Grier. Such films were pumped out by studios hungry for high box office returns on their modest production investments.

Most of these films are little more than time capsules in the twenty-first century. Yet blaxploitation served an important function in the early 1970s, according to critic Mike Phillips: "The characters talked like street people, they dressed the way you could see people dressed any Saturday night. . . . There was a realism that seemed to offer a new value to black manners and issues."[99]

Author Ed Guerrero disagrees, claiming that such movies only set black audiences' tastes to a "uniformly low standard. Thus blaxploitation movies marginalized any effort by independent black filmmakers to portray African American life in socially or politically relevant or human terms."[100]

One filmmaker who steered clear of the popular genre was Charles Burnett. Born in Mississippi but raised in Watts, Burnett began making films in the late 1960s. But it was his third work, 1977's *Killer of Sheep*, that first drew widespread attention. Ironically, the movie was never meant for widespread release. Yet its story of a working-class black family has gained legendary status over the years. The film is a "visual poem," says *New York Times* critic Manohla Dargis, filled with "the jazz and moody blues that seep into your head like smoke."[101]

Beloved Purple: The Novel Returns

During the black arts movement, the primary means of artistic expressions were poetry, drama, and music. Yet fiction never completely went away. Novelists such as Hal Bennett and Henry Dumas published important work in the 1960s and 1970s, but the mass appeal of novels did not return until the black arts movement was officially dead.

Two of the most important writers to emerge after the end of the black arts movement were Toni Morrison and Alice Walker. While only a handful of women received wide acclaim during the movement's heyday, Morrison and Walker found wide acceptance and popularity with both black and white audiences.

Morrison, for one, recognized the importance of the black arts movement's vision. Yet the former book editor never directly involved herself. "I think all good art has always been political. Art becomes a mere soapbox not because it's too political but because the artist isn't any good at what he's doing"[102]

Morrison forged a unique and powerful body of work. Her novels *Sula, The Bluest Eye,* and *Beloved* are considered modern classics. In 1993 Morrison became the first African American to be awarded the Nobel Prize in Literature, considered the highest award any writer can receive.

Kwanzaa

In the mid-1960s university professor Maulana Karenga founded Us, a black nationalist group that rivaled the Black Panthers. Karenga led his own demonstrations and developed his own ideas on black power. Yet today Karenga is best known as the creator of Kwanzaa, a yearly celebration of African traditions. Taken from the Swahili phrase *matunda ya kwanzaa*, meaning "first fruits," Kwanzaa is based on the ancient harvest rituals of Egypt and Nubia. Each year, many African Americans set aside December 26 to January 1 as a time to share with family. Often, traditional African clothes are worn and candles are lit as loved ones gather for a feast consisting of African delicacies. Gifts for children must include a book and a heritage symbol—a commitment to history and tradition.

Since its inception, Kwanzaa's popularity has only grown. Yet unlike other winter holidays such as Christmas and Hanukkah, it is not a religious celebration. Instead, says Karenga, "Kwanzaa brings a cultural message which speaks to the best of what it means to be African and human in the fullest sense."

Maulana Karenga, "The Founder's Welcome," The Official Kwanzaa Web Site. www.officialkwanzaa website.org.

A black American and his son light candles as part of the traditions of Kwanzaa.

Alice Walker also found mainstream literary success in the years following the demise of the black arts movement. Her best-known novel, 1982's *The Color Purple*, centers on a poor, abused woman named Celie who, after being raped by her stepfather, is married off to a brutal man, referred to only as Mister. For years after, Celie writes to God about her pain. She is most heart stricken by the separation from her dear sister, Nettie, who has found a new life in Africa. *The Color Purple* won Walker a Pulitzer Prize and a National Book Award. Yet Walker, unlike Morrison, almost completely distanced herself from the legacy of the black arts movement, says biographer Evelyn C. White: "Having written a novel in which the theme of black accountability superseded the racism of whites . . . Alice was clearly not in step with Black Arts ideology."[103]

Yet in spite of Walker's tacit rejection, a host of black artists did embrace the basic tenets of the black arts and black power movements. As the twentieth century drew to a close, legions of young musicians, poets, novelists, and dramatists heard the call. They embraced the best—and sometimes the worst—aspects of the black arts movement, forging new messages for a new generation and pushing "blackness" and black voices into the mainstream of American life.

Epilogue

The Legacy

The End/The Beginning

As black power lost its grip on the nation in 1975, artists of color continued creating but did so without an official movement behind them. Then again, black arts had always been less a single entity than a collection of artists and intellectuals working toward the common goals of unity, liberation, and self-reliance. Black arts promoted the recognition that "the souls of black folk were valuable, worthy, even sacred,"[104] writes William L. Van Deburg. By fusing the artist and the community, a unique and potentially transformative bond was formed.

As for one of the movement's leaders, the passing of black arts served only as an important step on a lifelong journey. In 1974, the former LeRoi Jones, Amiri Baraka, renounced black nationalism in favor of Marxism. From that time on, Baraka focused his attention more globally on native African peoples and their struggle for liberation. For some in the black arts movement, this shift was a betrayal of the cause. But, according to author Jerry Gafio Watts, "Baraka claimed to have intensified his commitment to the emancipation of black America, arguing that Marxism was the logical next step for any sound thinking, revolutionary, Black Nationalist."[105]

More recently, Baraka stoked controversy again. In 2001, while serving a term as New Jersey's poet laureate, he wrote the poem "Somebody Blew Up America." A response to the terrorist attacks of September 11 that left more than three thousand people dead, the poem contained a passage that has since become infamous in which Baraka asked who knew of the imminent attacks. His strong suspicion, the poem implies, is that the Israeli government of Ariel Sharon did. Israel has long been an ally of the United States. Was Baraka's idea of a possible conspiracy well founded, or was his poem simply an example of what critics had for years called his latent anti-Semitism, or what he refers to as anti-Zionism?

For then-governor of New Jersey James McGreevey, such distinctions made no difference. Although he could not legally remove Baraka from his post as state poet laureate, in 2003 McGreevey convinced New Jersey legislators to abolish the honor.

But Baraka's continuing outspokenness is only one part of the black power and black arts legacy. It is a legacy that extends beyond traditional poetry, music, and drama. "Black Power quickly came to mean very different things to different people," says historian Manning Marable. "For black entrepreneurs who manipulated blackness to sell goods and services in poor urban communities, Black Power was a demand to control black consumer markets."[106]

Thus as the influence of black arts dimmed, consumerism, typically in the form of rap and hip-hop music, rose up to take its place. Throughout the late 1970s and early 1980s, rappers such as Kurtis Blow, Run DMC, and Sugar Hill Gang produced albums that spoke of inner city black life with a sense of street credibility that black (and white) youth responded to. The 1983 rap record *White Lines* by Melle Mel and Grandmaster Flash encouraged young people to avoid the temptations of cocaine with memorable lines and a danceable beat. Although such records would in time give way to heavier and more violent gangsta rap, many artists carried on black arts' tradition of revolution.

Fight the Power

Perhaps the most influential rap outfit of the late 1980s and early 1990s was Long Island's Public Enemy, led by Chuck D and Flavor Flav. Their unique brand of politically conscious rap and their devotion to black communities had long been popular with inner city African Americans. Albums such as *Yo! Bum Rush the Show* in 1987 and *It Takes a Nation of Millions to Hold Us Back* a year later owed much in the way of articulation and attitude to the black arts movement.

But it was not until Spike Lee's *Do the Right Thing* that Public Enemy's music reached the rest of the world. Released in 1989 amid newspaper accounts of racial violence in Brooklyn and set

Writer/director Spike Lee, left, starred in and directed his ground-breaking film on race relations in *Do the Right Thing* in 1989.

on the hottest day of the year, Lee's film centers on white pizza parlor owner Sal and his two sons. As the sole white business owners in the neighborhood, the men argue over their minority status. Their delivery guy, Mookie (played by the director), acts as a thorn in their sides. Later, he and his black friends become a catalyst for the story's climactic violence. Images of Malcolm X and Martin Luther King linger over the film, asking the unspoken question first posed years before: Is violence useful or not in gaining one's rights?

Played throughout *Do the Right Thing* is Public Enemy's song "Fight the Power," which rails against white dominated music and the so-called heroes of the white world. Public Enemy's sentiments soon gained a wide following.

American Legacy: Black Arts in the Twenty-first Century

American popular culture is now awash in more images of African Americans than ever before. "If Black Power influenced urban youth," says Peniel E. Joseph, "the Black Arts enjoyed their own renaissance through the popularity of hip-hop-inflected poetry slams and organized tributes to cultural icons, including Sonia Sanchez, Nikki Giovanni, Askia Touré, and Amiri Baraka."[107]

In the world of drama, August Wilson's work has few peers, regardless of color. In 2005, only months before his death, Wilson completed his Century Cycle of ten plays, each representing a decade of the twentieth century. From the father-son relationship of *Fences* to the struggle over a family heirloom in *The Piano Lesson*, Wilson succeeded in putting black people on stage, living the complexity of the African American experience through flawed, human characters. Although he was not the first black dramatist, many critics agree that Wilson's ambition and vision put him in the front ranks of American literature.

Black poets, novelists, and musical artists also continue flourishing. "Today's black arts scene," writes Henry Louis Gates, "is characterized by an awareness of previous black traditions that the new artists self-consciously echo, imitate, parody and revise in acts of 'riffing' or 'signifying' or even 'sampling.'"[108]

Such sampling is both an homage to past artists and a look forward, as novelists, musicians, dancers, and painters build new monuments to the complexity and beauty of human experience. But unlike the work of the black arts movement, the creations invite all people, regardless of color, to look and listen. The politics are still there, the struggle for equality and understanding continues, yet "today's African American artists increasingly strike themes that are racially and culturally universal,"[109] says writer Jack E. White. From wider cultural acceptance comes a deeper confidence. Langston Hughes's words, now almost a century old, still speak for a new generation: "We younger Negro artists who create now intend to express our individual, dark-skinned selves without fear or shame. We build our temples for tomorrow, strong as we know how, and we stand on top of the mountain, free within ourselves."[110]

Beyond Malcolm

Like most legends, the birth of the black arts movement following the death of Malcolm X contains seeds of truth and a host of misconceptions. Yet one thing is certain: The black arts movement continues influencing contemporary American culture. Echoes of it reside in the socially conscious hip-hop/funk of artists like the Roots, whose early album title *Things Fall Apart* is taken from Nigerian writer Chinua Achebe's novel of the same name, as well as the novels and stories of Edward P. Jones, Pulitzer Prize–winning author of *The Known World*.

"The mission," says Haki Madhubuti, "is how do we become a whole people, tell our story?"[111] Madhubuti does not suggest a complete answer. Yet what is clear is that today more people of all ethnicities want to listen, share in, sympathize with, and understand the African American experience. The true legacy of the black arts movement is still evolving, yet before long the revolution that the black arts began may become unnecessary. "If the mission of these black artists succeeds," writes Gates, "the very need to declare a 'renaissance' . . . may be unnecessary, which means that today's may truly be the renaissance to end all renaissances."[112]

Notes

Introduction: "Recapture Our Heritage"

1. Quoted in Alex Haley, *The Autobiography of Malcolm X*. New York: Ballantine, 1973, p. 175.

2. Quoted in David Farber and Beth Bailey, *The Columbia Guide to America in the 1960s*. New York: Columbia University Press, 2001, p. 61.

3. James Edward Smethurst, *The Black Arts Movement: Literary Nationalism in the 1960s and 1970s*. Chapel Hill and London: University of North Carolina Press, 2005, p. 25.

4. Henry Louis Gates, "Black Creativity: On the Cutting Edge," *Time*, October 10, 1994. www.time.com.

5. Gates, "Black Creativity."

Chapter One: The Roots of Black Nationalism

6. Quoted in Adam Hochschild, *Bury the Chains: Prophets and Rebels in the Fight to Free an Empire's Slaves*. Boston: Mariner, 2006, p. 32.

7. Charles George, *Life Under the Jim Crow Laws*. San Diego: Lucent, 2000, p. 10.

8. Quoted in PBS, *Marcus Garvey: Look for Me in the Whirlwind*. www.pbs.org/wgbh/amex/garvey/filmmore/pt.html.

9. Quoted in PBS, *Marcus Garvey*.

10. Quoted in Aggrey Brown, *Color, Class, and Politics in Jamaica*. Piscataway, New Jersey: Rutgers, 1980,

11. Quoted in PBS, *Marcus Garvey*.

12. Quoted in PBS, *Marcus Garvey*.

13. Quoted in PBS, *Marcus Garvey*.

14. Harvard Sitkoff, *The Struggle for Black Equality: 1954–1980*. New York: Hill and Wang, 1981, p. 10.

15. Quoted in PBS, *Marcus Garvey*.

16. Smethurst, *The Black Arts Movement*, p. 110.

17. Quoted in Robert J. Norrell, *The House I Live In: Race in the American Century*. Oxford: Oxford University Press, 2005, p. 96.

18. Robert J. Norrell, *The House I Live In*, p. 97.

19. Lang;ston Hughes, "The Negro Artist and the Racial Mountain," *Nation*, June 23, 1926. www.thenation.com.

20. Hughes, "The Negro Artist and the Racial Mountain."

21. Ralph Ellison, *Invisible Man*. New York: Vintage, 1981, p. 3.

22. Quoted in David Farber and Beth Bailey, *The Columbia Guide to America in the 1960s*, p. 48.

Chapter Two: The Rise of the Black Arts Movement

23. Quoted in Haley, *The Autobiography of Malcolm X*, p. 432.

24. Quoted in Haley, *The Autobiography of Malcolm X*, p. 434.

25. Quoted in Haley, *The Autobiography of Malcolm X*, p. 434.

26. Quoted in Haley, *The Autobiography of Malcolm X*, p. 435.

27. Amiri Baraka, *The Autobiography of LeRoi Jones*. New York: Freundlich, 1984, p. 202.

28. Baraka, *The Autobiography of LeRoi Jones*, p. 202.

29. Baraka, *The Autobiography of LeRoi Jones*, p. 202.

30. Quoted in Peniel E. Joseph, *Waiting 'til the Midnight Hour: A Narrative History of Black Power in America*. New York: Holt, 2006, p. 256.

31. Baraka, *The Autobiography of LeRoi Jones*, p. 212.

32. Smethurst, *The Black Arts Movement*, p. 103.

33. Smethurst, *The Black Arts Movement*, p. 106.

34. Quoted in Julius E. Thompson, *Dudley Randall, Broadside Press, and the Black Arts Movement in Detroit, 1960–1995*. Jefferson, NC: McFarland, 2005, p. 149.

35. Quoted in National Public Radio, *Tell Me More: Wisdom Watch*, November 21, 2007. www.npr.org.

36. Quoted in National Public Radio, *Tell Me More*.

37. Quoted in Floyd W. Hayes III et al., eds., *A Turbulent Voyage: Readings in African American Studies*. Lanham, MD: Rowman and Littlefield, 2000, p. 237.

38. Quoted in National Public Radio, *Tell Me More*.

39. George Breitman, "In Defense of Black Power," *International Socialist Review*, January–February 1967.

40. Breitman, "In Defense of Black Power."

41. Quoted in Valerie Reitman and Mitchell Lansberg, "Watts Riots, 40 Years Later," *Los Angeles Times*, August 11, 2005. www.latimes.com.

42. Quoted in Reitman and Lansberg, "Watts Riots, 40 Years Later."

Chapter Three: Cultural Influences and Identity

43. Manning Marable, *Living Black History*. New York: Basic Civitas Books, 2006, p. 96.

44. Quoted in Ebere Onwudiwe and Minabere Ibelema, eds., *Afro-Optimism: Perspectives on Africa's Advances*. Oxford, UK: Greenwood, 2002, pp. 55–56.

45. Quoted in Michael L. Krenn, *Fall-Out Shelters for the Human Spirit: American Art and the Cold War*. Chapel Hill: University of North Carolina Press, 2005, p. 187.

46. Larry Neal, "The Black Writer's Role," *Liberator*, June 1966, p. 8.

47. Quoted in Frantz Fanon, *The Wretched of the Earth*. New York: Grove, 1968, cover.

48. Fanon, *The Wretched of the Earth*, p. 39.

49. Fanon, *The Wretched of the Earth*, p. 94.

50. Quoted in Hayes, *A Turbulent Voyage*, p. 237.

51. LeRoi Jones, *Blues People: Negro Music in White America*. New York: William Morrow, 1999, introduction.

52. Geoffrey C. Ward, *Jazz: A History of America's Music*. New York: Knopf, 2000, p. 413.

53. Quoted in Ward, *Jazz*, p. 413.

54. Quoted in Ward, *Jazz*, p. 434.

55. Quoted in Ward, *Jazz*, p. 436.

56. Quoted in Ward, *Jazz*, p. 436.

57. Quoted in Howard Dodson, *Jubilee: The Emergence of African-American Culture*. Washington, DC: National Geographic, 2002, p. 186.

58. Nina Simone and Stephen Cleary, *I Put a Spell on You: The Autobiography of Nina Simone*. New York: Da Capo, 2003, p. 89.

59. Joseph, *Waiting 'til the Midnight Hour*, p. 55.

60. Joseph, *Waiting 'til the Midnight Hour*, p. 56.

61. Quoted in Joseph, *Waiting 'til the Midnight Hour*, p. 55.

62. Quoted in Joseph, *Waiting 'til the Midnight Hour*, p. 90.

Chapter Four: Assimilation or Self-Determination?

63. Quoted in Hayes, *A Turbulent Voyage*, p. 237.

64. Jerry Gafio Watts, *Amiri Baraka: The Politics and Art of a Black Intellectual*. New York: New York University Press, 2001, p. 201.

65. Quoted in Watts, *Amiri Baraka*, p. 201.

66. Quoted in Watts, *Amiri Baraka*, p. 201.

67. Quoted in Fritz Gysin and Christopher Mulvey, *Black Liberation in America*. Berlin: LIT Verlag Berlin, 2001, p. 203.

68. Quoted in PBS, *Eyes on the Prize: Power! (1966–1968)*. www.pbs.org.

69. Quoted in British Broadcasting Corporation, "1968: Black Athletes Make Silent Protest," October 17, 2005. http://news.bbc.co.uk.

70. Quoted in British Broadcasting Corporation, "1968."

71. Quoted in Sitkoff, *The Struggle for Black Equality*, p. 217.

72. Quoted in PBS, *Eyes on the Prize: Power! (1966–1968)*.

73. Quoted in Harry J. Elam and David Krasner, eds., *African American Performance and Theater History: A Critical Reader*. New York:

Oxford University Press USA, 2000, p. 56.

74. Quoted in Elam and Krasner, *African American Performance and Theater History*, pp. 56–57.

75. Quoted in PBS, *Eyes on the Prize: Power! (1966–1968)*.

76. Robert J. Norrell, *The House I Live In: Race in the American Century*. Oxford: Oxford University Press, 2005, pp. 262–63.

77. Quoted in PBS, *Eyes on the Prize: Power! (1966–1968)*.

78. Joseph, *Waiting 'til the Midnight Hour*, p. 214.

79. Joseph, *Waiting 'til the Midnight Hour*, p. 215.

80. Joseph, *Waiting 'til the Midnight Hour*, p. 216.

81. Henry Louis Gates, *Thirteen Ways of Looking at a Black Man*. New York: Vintage, 1997, p. 24.

82. Quoted in PBS, *Eyes on the Prize: Two Societies (1965–1968)*. www.pbs.org.

83. Baraka, *The Autobiography of LeRoi Jones*, p. 215.

Chapter Five: Black Arts Hit the Mainstream

84. Quoted in PBS, *Eyes on the Prize: Ain't Gonna Shuffle No More (1964–1968)*. www.pbs.org.

85. Quoted in *Eyes on the Prize: Ain't Gonna Shuffle No More (1964–1968)*.

86. Quoted in *Eyes on the Prize: Ain't Gonna Shuffle No More (1964–1968)*.

87. Quoted in *Eyes on the Prize: Ain't Gonna Shuffle No More (1964–1968)*.

88. Quoted in *Eyes on the Prize: Ain't Gonna Shuffle No More (1964–1968)*.

89. Quoted in Dodson, *Jubilee*, p. 187.

90. William L. Van Deburg, *Black Camelot: African-American Culture Heroes in Their Times, 1960–1980*. Chicago: University of Chicago Press, 1997, p. 73.

91. Joseph, *Waiting 'til the Midnight Hour*, pp. 256–57.

92. Gil Scott-Heron, "The Revolution Will Not Be Televised," *Pieces of a Man*, RCA Records, 1971.

93. Mark Anthony Neal, *What the Music Said: Black Popular Music and Black Public Culture*. New York: Routledge, 1998, p. 107.

94. Jeffrey O.G. Ogbar, *Black Power: Radical Politics and African American Identity*. Baltimore: Johns Hopkins University Press, 2005, p. 111.

95. Baraka, *The LeRoi Jones/Amiri Baraka Reader*, p. 369.

96. Quoted in African American Cinema Gallery, "The Roots of Black Cinema." www.black-cinema.org.

97. Quoted in S. Torriano Berry, *The 50 Most Influential Black Films*. New York: Citadel, 2000, p. 123.

98. Donald Bogle, *Toms, Coons, Mulattoes, Mammies, and Bucks: An Inter*

pretive History of Blacks in American Films. New York: Continuum, 2003, p. 239.

99. Quoted in Francesca T. Royster, *Becoming Cleopatra: The Shifting Image of an Icon.* New York: Palgrave/Macmillan, 2003, p. 155.

100. Ed Guerrero, *Framing Blackness: The African American Image in Film.* Philadelphia: Temple University Press, 1993, p. 104.

101. Manohla Dargis, "Whereabouts in Watts? Where Poetry Meets Chaos," *New York Times*, March 30, 2007. www.nytimes.com.

102. Quoted in Danille Taylor-Guthrie, ed., *Conversations with Toni Morrison.* Jackson: University Press of Mississippi, 1994, p. 3.

103. Evelyn C. White, *Alice Walker: A Life.* New York: Norton, 2005, p. 196.

Epilogue: Legacy

104. William L. Van Deburg, *New Day in Babylon: The Black Power Movement and American Culture.* Chicago: University of Chicago Press, 1993, p. 186.

105. Watts, *Amiri Baraka*, p. 423.

106. Manning Marable, *Speaking Truth to Power: Essays on Race, Resistance, and Radicalism.* New York: Perseus, 1998, p. 7.

107. Joseph, *Waiting 'til the Midnight Hour*, p. 297.

108. Gates, "Black Creativity."

109. Jack E. White, "The Beauty of Black Art," *Time*, October 10, 1994. www.time.com.

110. Hughes, "The Negro Artist and the Racial Mountain."

111. Quoted in National Public Radio, *Tell Me More.*

112. Gates, "Black Creativity."

For More Information

The brevity of this book makes it impossible to include all of the people, events, and ideas of the black arts and black power movements. The sources below are meant to further your exploration of this and other fascinating periods of American history.

Books

Howard Dodson, *Jubilee: The Emergence of African American Culture*. Washington, DC: National Geographic, 2003. This large and lovely coffee-table book celebrates the arts, crafts, and literature made by African Americans over the last four centuries. Archival drawings as well as full-color photographs are mixed with contemporary expressions of the black experience. Noted African Americans add their words to Dodson's historical overview.

Jim Haskins, *Power to the People: The Rise and Fall of the Black Panther Party*. New York: Simon & Schuster, 1997. For students looking for more information on the Black Panthers, there is no better place to start than this thorough and well-researched volume. Learn more about the people and events that shaped the most controversial black organization in U.S. history.

Laurel Holliday, *Dreaming in Color, Living in Black and White: Our Own Stories of Growing Up Black in America*. New York: Simon Pulse, 2000. Author Holliday interviews seventeen African Americans, from teens to seniors. Each person recounts the most important racial experiences—some cruel, many painful—of their lives. The book is an invaluable firsthand look at race, class, and other issues that divide Americans.

Web Sites

Amiri Baraka: Official Web site (www. amiribaraka.com). One of the prime movers and shakers of the black arts movement runs his own Web site. Check it out to explore Baraka's books and essays, sound clips of his poems and speeches, and a gallery of photographs.

Blaxploitation.com (www.blaxploita tion.com). This loving tribute site will tell you all you need to know about the blaxploitation films of the 1960s and 1970s. Whether you are seeking *Foxy Brown, Black Jesus, Sweet Sweetback*, or *Thomasine and Bushrod*, the site boasts articles, book titles, posters, and soundtrack information and is dedicated to "folks who've had enough of the man."

Library of Congress: American Memory (http://memory.loc.gov/ ammem/index.html). The world's supreme contemporary library curates a fascinating online exhibition on the continuing history of African Americans. This exhaustive site contains reproductions of historic documents, as well as slave narratives and a portion devoted to Jackie Robinson, the man who broke the color barrier in baseball.

Malcolm X (www.brothermalcolm.net). University of Toledo sociology professor Abdul Alkalimat is the developer of this comprehensive site dedicated to the life and work of Malcolm X. Speeches, photographs, and a teacher's study guide are just a few of the resources you will find here. This is an in-depth and well-organized historical look at the black leader.

Third World Press (www.thirdworld pressinc.com). Buy more books! One place to begin is Third World Press, the largest independent black-owned publishing house in the United States, and also one of the oldest. Still run from offices in Chicago by black arts pioneer Haki Madhubuti, Third World publishes the work of many authors of color, including poet Gwendolyn Brooks and commentator Tavis Smiley.

Zora Neale Hurston (www.zoraneale hurston.com). Get started exploring the life and work of one of the greatest writers of the Harlem Renaissance. This charming site includes a biography, teacher resources, and information on Hurston's descendant Lucy Anne, who travels the country spreading her aunt's legacy.

Museums

The African American Museum in Philadelphia (www.aampmuseum. org). Known as the first of its kind in the United States, the African American Museum in Philadelphia includes four galleries of exhibitions and artifacts, along with frequent dance and music performances. The history of African Americans is charted from the slave trade through the present day. A recent exhibition, Inside the Struggle: Civil Rights and the Philadelphia Connection, is a highlight.

Frederick Douglass: National Historic Site (www.nps.gov/frdo). Located in the Anacostia section of Washington, D.C., Cedar Hill was the nineteenth-century leader's last home. Visitors can view a brief film on Douglass's life and tour the mansion, where you will find his desk, beloved violin, and the many gifts he accrued over his life, including ones given to him by President Abraham Lincoln and novelist Harriet Beecher Stowe. Go online for a virtual tour of the premises.

The National Civil Rights Museum (www.civilrightsmuseum.org). For an encounter with American history like no other, visit the National Civil Rights Museum in Memphis, Tennessee. Built from the old Lorraine Motel, the museum houses a variety of exhibits, many of which you can touch and experience up close. From the Voices of Struggle display to a Montgomery, Alabama, bus almost identical to the one on which Rosa Parks sat, visitors can virtually live the struggle. The touching final stop

on the tour is the preserved motel room where Martin Luther King stayed the night before his murder in April 1968.

Albums

John Coltrane, *A Love Supreme*. Considered by critics to be Coltrane's masterpiece, the album, Coltrane said, is a tribute to God. Released in 1964, it influenced not only other jazz musicians but a generation of rock artists like Jimi Hendrix and Cream.

Public Enemy, *Fear of a Black Planet*. Public Enemy's raw third album is in-your-face, political rap. Aside from the infamous songs "911 Is a Joke" and "Fight the Power," the record boasts nineteen others tracks filled with urgency and anger. Leader Chuck D and sidekick Flavor Flav are often called the granddaddies of modern rap. Listen and understand why. Warning: explicit lyrics.

Stevie Wonder, *Innervisions*. Wonder's 1973 release is a perfect fusion of soul music and black arts activism. Evocative, socially conscious songs like "Living for the City" and "Higher Ground" are mixed with plaintive ballads, including "All in Love Is Fair." *Innervisions* is not only of its time but of all time.

Index

actors, 22, 77, 78
Africa
  culture of
    celebration of, 44, 46
    loss during slavery of, 12
  Garvey supporters and, 18
  Harlem Renaissance and, 21
  slave trade in, 13
Afros (hairstyles), 70–71
Algeria, 48
Angelou, Maya, 76
art, slave, 15
assimilation, 14, 17–18, 45

Bailey, Joseph, 18
Baraka, Amiri
  black nationalism renounced by, 83
  on Coltrane, 53
  on expressing soul, 72
  on importance of Black Arts Movement, 68
  name chosen by, 57
  as New Jersey poet laureate, 83–84
  Sun Ra and, 31
  See also Jones, LeRoi
beauty, 69–72
Benjamin X, 29
Birmingham, Alabama church bombing, 54
Black, Fred, 70
"Black Art" (Jones), 42

Black Arts Movement
  black criticism of, 58–59
  importance of, 10–11, 68, 87
  overview of, 9–10
  popular culture and, 77, 86, 87
"Black Arts Movement, The" (Neal), 57–58
Black Arts Repertory Theatre and School (BARTS), 30, 32–33, 56
Black Boy (Wright), 37
Black Day in July (Lightfoot), 41
Black Fire (Jones and Neal), 32
Black House, 65–66
black institutions and leadership and, 39–40
  entrepreneurs and, 84
  overview of, 9
  soul and, 72–74
  violence and, 40, 49
  See also black nationalism
black nationalism
  arts and, 57–58, 63
  beliefs of, 27
  Black Arts Movement and, 9–10
  described, 12
  renounced by Baraka, 83
Black Panther Party, 58
Black Panther Party for Self-Defense, 62–63, 65
black power movement, 9, 68, 90
black pride, 58, 69–72, 81

Black Scholar (journal), 67

Black Student (magazine), 48

black studies programs, 65–68

"Black University Manifesto, The" (Hare), 67

Blaxploitation, 75, 78–80

"blk/rhetoric" (Sanchez), 36

Blues People: Negro Music in America (Jones), 50

Brackett, Nathan, 75

Breitman, George, 39–40

Broadside Press, 36, 39

Brooks, Gwendolyn, 52

Brown v. Board of Education, 26

Bullins, Ed, 33, 65

Burnett, Charles, 80

Carlos, John, 61

Carmichael, Stokely, 59, 61, 62

Césaire, Aimé, 48

"Change Is Gonna Come, A" (Cooke), 72

Chuck D, 84

churches, 54–55

civil rights movement, 26–27, 55

Cleage, Albert, 54–55, 68

Cleaver, Eldridge, 64, 65

Clifton, Lucille, 76

Coleman, Ornette, 50

colonialism, 16, 39, 46–49

Color Purple, The (Morrison), 82

Coltrane, Alice, 53

Coltrane, John, 50, 53

composers. See musicians

Cooke, Sam, 72

Cosby, Bill, 77

Crisis (magazine), 45

Crisis of the Negro Intellectual (Cruse), 32

Cruse, Harold, 32

Damas, Léon, 48

Davis, Miles, 50, 53

Detroit, 41, 74

Do the Right Thing (film), 85–86

Douglass, Frederick, 15

DuBois, W.E.B.

   assimilation policies of, 14, 17

   background of, 45

   Nigger Heaven and, 23

   Pan-Africanism and, 43

Dunbar, Paul Lawrence, 21

Dutchman (Jones), 30

Ellison, Ralph, 24

entrepreneurs, 84

Equino, Olaudah, 13–14

Eugenides, Jeffrey, 41

Fanon, Frantz, 46–49

Fetchit, Stepin, 77

field Negroes, 39

"Fight the Power" (Public Enemy), 86

filmmakers, 77–80, 86

Flavor Flav, 84

Flowers for the Trash-man (Marvin X), 65–66

For Malcolm (anthology), 36

France, 48–49

Friends of Negro Freedom, 20

Frye, Marquette, 40

Frye, Rena, 40

Frye, Ronald, 40

Fuller, Charles, 35

Funnyhouse of a Negro (Kennedy), 35

Galamison (reverend), 29
Garvey, Marcus, 14–20
Gates, Henry Louis
  on black studies programs, 66, 68
  on current state of black arts, 86–87
  on purpose of Black Arts Movement,
    11
  on success of black artists, 87
Gaye, Marvin, 75–76
George, Charles, 14
Giddings, Paula, 71
Giovanni, Nikki, 35–36, 66, 68
Goin' a Buffalo (Bullins), 33
Goncalves, Joe, 58
Gordy, Berry, 74
Gregory, Robin, 70–71
Guerrero, Ed, 80

hairstyles, 70–71
Hansberry, Lorraine, 60
Hare, Nathan, 67
Harlem, New York, 30, 33
Harlem Renaissance, 20–26, 55
Hayes, Isaac, 78
Hill, Robert, 15
Holiday, Billie, 72
"Homage to My Hips" (Clifton),
  76
Hooks, Bell, 64
house Negroes, 39
Howard University, 67, 70–71
Howells, William Dean, 21
Hughes, Langston, 20, 23, 24, 87
Hurston, Nora Zeale, 25

"If We Must Die" (McKay), 23
I Know Why the Caged Bird Sings
  (Angelou), 76
"In Defense of Black Power," 39–40
Innervisions (Wonder), 74
Institute for Positive Education, 38
integration, 26
intellectuals
  black studies programs, 65–68
  Cruse, 32
  Du Bois, 14, 17, 23, 43, 45
  Fanon, 46–49
  Gates, 11, 66, 68, 86–87
  Hare, 67
  Hughes, 20–21, 23, 24, 87
  Johnson, 20–21
  Soul on Ice and white, 64
  See also Neal, Larry
Invisible Man (Ellison), 26

Jackmon, Marvin, 65–66
Jacquette, Tommy, 40, 42
jazz, 33, 50, 53, 72
Jim Crow laws, 14, 18
Johnson, James Weldon, 20–21
Johnson, Slyvia, 56
Jones, Hettie, 30
Jones, LeRoi
  assassination of Malcolm X and, 28–29
  BARTS and, 30, 32–33
  black studies programs and, 66
  increasing commitment to black cul-
    ture, 56–57
  Spirit House, 33
  study of roots of American music, 50
  See also Baraka, Amiri

Joseph, Peniel F.
  on Black Arts Movement influence on
    popular culture, 86
  on Black House, 66
  on black recording industry, 74
  on black studies programs, 66
  on Cleage, 54
  on LeRoi Jones, 66
Journal of Negro Poetry, 58

Karenga, Maulana, 81
Kennedy, Adrienne, 35
Killer of Sheep (film), 80
King, Martin Luther, Jr., 8, 26
King, Woodie, Jr., 35
Kwanzaa, 81

Latimore, Jewel C., 36
Lee, Don. *See* Madhubuti, Haki
Lee, Spike, 85–86
Lightfoot, Gordon, 41
Little, Malcolm. *See* Malcolm X
"Living for the City" (Wonder), 74
Locke, Alain, 23
Long March, 13
Love Supreme, A (Coltrane), 53

Macbeth, Robert, 33
Madhubuti, Haki, 36–38, 87
Majors and Minors (Dunbar), 21
Malcolm X
  assassination of, 28–30
  beliefs of, 8–9, 27, 55
  names of, 38
Marable, Manning, 43, 84
Marvin X, 65–66

Marxism, 49, 83
"Mask, The" (Dunbar), 21
Mayfield, Curtis, 75
McDaniel, Hattie, 77
McGreevey, James, 84
McKay, Claude, 23
Mencken, H.L., 21
Messenger (magazine), 17
Micheaux, Oscar, 77
Middle Passage, 13
Middlesex (Eugenides), 41
Mills, Charles, 18
Minikus, Lee, 40
Morrison, Toni, 80, 82
Motown, 74–76
Mules and Men (Hurston), 25
musicians
  benefits to white, 50
  Coleman, 50
  Coltrane, 51, 53
  Cooke, 72
  Davis, 50, 53
  Hayes, 78
  Holiday, 72
  Mayfield, 75
  Motown, 74–76
  rap, 84–86
  Robeson, 22
  slave, 15
  Sun Ra, 31, 53

National Association for the Advancement of Colored People (NAACP),
  48–49
National Black Theatre, 34
National Liberation Front (FLN), 48–49

Neal, Larry
  background of, 32
  BARTS and, 32–33
  on black arts and nationalism and
    self-determination, 57–58
  Black Panthers and, 58, 62
  on black power, 39, 49
  on importance of symbols, 59
  on World Festival of Negro Arts,
    46
Neal, Mark Anthony, 74
negritude movement, 48
"Negro Artist and the Racial Mountain,
  The" (Hughes), 24
"Negro Speaks of Rivers, A" (Hughes),
  20, 72
Negro World (newspaper), 18
New Federal Theatre, 35
New Lafayette Theatre, 33–34
New Negro, The (Locke), 23
New Negro movement. See Harlem
  Renaissance
Newton, Huey, 62, 65
Nigger Heaven (Van Vechten), 23
nonfiction writers, 76
  See also intellectuals
Norrell, Robert J., 21, 65
novelists
  Ellison, 24
  Hurston, 25
  Morrison, 80, 82
  Reed, 58
  Walker, 82
  Wright, 37

Oak and Ivy (Dunbar), 21

Ogbar, Jeffrey O.G., 76
Olympic Games (1968, Mexico City), 61
O'Neal, William, 63, 65

Pan-Africanism, 43–44
Parks, Gordon, 78
Parks, Gordon, Jr., 78
Parks, Rosa, 26
philosophers. See intellectuals
playwrights
  Bullins, 33, 65
  Fuller, 35
  Hansberry, 60
  Kennedy, 35
  King, Woodie, Jr., 35
  Marvin X, 65–66
  Wilson, 86
  See also Baraka, Amiri; Jones, LeRoi
poets
  Brooks, 52
  Clifton, 76
  Dunbar, 21
  Giovanni, 35–36, 66, 68
  Hughes, 20, 23, 24, 87
  Madhubuti, 36–38
  McKay, 23
  Reed, 58
  Sanchez, 35–36, 66, 69–70, 72
  Scott-Heron, 74
  slave, 15
  See also Baraka, Amiri; Jones, LeRoi
Poitier, Sidney, 77
Public Enemy, 84–85, 86
publishers, 36–39

race riots, 23, 40–42

racism, 14, 18, 48–49

Raison in the Sun, A (Hansberry), 60

Randall, Dudley, 36, 38

Randolph, A. Philip, 17, 20

reconciliation. *See* assimilation

recording industry, 74–77

Red Summer, 23

Reed, Ishmael, 58

religion, 54–55

Rerrie, Joyce, 14–15

Richards, Lloyd, 60

Robeson, Paul, 22

Rodgers, Carolyn, 36

Rose, Philip, 60

Sanchez, Sonia
  on beauty, 69–70, 72
  black studies programs and, 66
  inspiration for poetry of, 35
  search for heroes by, 36

San Francisco State University (California), 66–68

Scott, Stanley, 30

Scott-Heron, Gil, 74

Seale, Bobby, 62, 65

self-determination
  arts and, 57–58
  assassinations of King and Malcolm X and, 56
  Black Arts Movement and, 38
  Garvey and, 17

Sell, Mike, 62–63

Senegal, 44

Senghor, Léopold Sédar, 48

Shabazz, El-Haji Malik el-. *See* Malcolm X

Shaft (film), 78

Simone, Nina, 54

Sitkoff, Harvard, 19

slavery, 12–14, 15, 39

Smethurst, James Edward
  on importance of Black Arts Movement, 11
  on importance of Garvey, 20
  on New Lafayette Theatre, 33
  on Woodie King Jr., 35

Smith, Tommie, 61

Snellings, Ronald, 66

Snipe, Tracy D., 44

Society of African Culture, 44

Soldier's Play, A (Fuller), 35

"Somebody Blew Up America" (Baraka), 84

soul music, 72–73

Souls of Black Folks, The (Du Bois), 43, 45

Soul on Ice (Cleaver), 64, 65

Soviet Union, 22

Spirit House, 33

"Steal Away" (song), 15

Street in Bronzeville, A (Brooks), 52

Student Nonviolent Coordinating Committee (SNCC), 59, 61

Sun Ra, 31, 53

Superfly (film), 75, 78

symbols, importance of, 59, 61

Teer, Barbara Ann, 34

theater, 30, 32–35

Their Eyes Were Watching God (Hurston), 25

Thiele, Bob, 74

Third World Press, 36, 39
"True Import of the Present Dialogue: Black vs. Negro, The" (Giovanni), 36

Umbra Writers Workshop, 58
Universal Negro Improvement Association (UNIA), 17–20
Up from Slavery (Washington), 17

Van Deburg, William L., 72, 83
Van Peebles, Melvin, 78
Van Vechten, Carl, 23, 24
violence
  Algerian independence movement and, 49
  black church and, 55
  Black Panthers and, 62–63, 65
  black power movement and, 40, 49
  Malcolm X and, 8
  opposition to, 8, 59, 61
  by whites, 23, 27, 54

Walker, Alice, 25, 82
Ward, Geoffrey C., 50
Washington, Booker T., 14, 17, 45
Watermelon Man (film), 78
Watts, Jerry Gafio, 58, 83
Watts riots, 40, 42
"What's Going On" (Gaye), 75–76

White, Evelyn C., 82
White, Jack E., 87
white Americans
  Black Panthers and, 63, 65
  fear of Garvey, 20
  media of, 62–63
  racism of
    Jim Crow laws, 14, 18
    violence and, 23, 27, 54
  supporters of black artists, 21, 24, 26
Wilson, August, 86
women
  actors, 77
  Angelou, 76
  musicians, 72
  novelists, 25, 80, 82
  playwrights, 35, 60
  poets
    Angelou, 76
    Brooks, 52
    Clifton, 76
    Giovanni, 35–36, 66, 68
    Sanchez, 35–36, 66, 69–70, 72
Wonder, Stevie, 74
World Festival of Negro Arts, 44, 46
Wretched of the Earth, The (Fanon), 46–48, 49
Wright, Richard, 37

Picture Credits

About the Author

David Robson is an award-winning writer and English professor. He is the recipient of a National Endowment for the Arts grant and two playwriting fellowships from the Delaware Division of the Arts. His love of words and stories was first inspired by his grandfather and, later, by the works of his favorite writers, including Langston Hughes. Robson lives with his wife and daughter in Wilmington, Delaware.